A Note from the Author

In this book I mention many tips and philosophies that I currently use in my daily life. I ask that you please consult your medical doctor to assure you are physically able to perform a daily exercise routine.

I don't guarantee anyone's success. Success is a very subjective term. I can guarantee that every word in this book has come from my heart.

These are opinions and are no substitute for professional services that may be administered by a doctor of psychology. Always consult a competent professional for answers to your specific questions.

I hope you find a few of my motivational methods useful in both your personal life and business life. Good luck and start getting in shape mentally and physically today—make it happen!

The Secret of Success:

"A Little Bit over a Long Period of Time"

By Phillip Crone

ISBN 13: 978-0-9774473-0-5
ISBN 10: 0-9774473-0-8

First Edition: January 2006

Designed and printed in the US by SelfPublishing.com

Acknowledgments

I want to thank my wife, Julia, and my daughters, Bailey and Rachel, for putting up with Dad's "keys to life sayings" over the past few years. Thank you for allowing me to reach my dreams and for giving me the best part of my life, my family. Without you as my sounding board, I would have not been able to formulate my many theories and ideals in life. You are all as much a part of this book as any idea that I might ever have. Thank you for being in my life and for your unconditional love and support.

I'd also like to thank Wiley Sword, noted Civil War author and neighbor, who has guided me during this project.

Special thanks to my fraternity brothers of Phi Sigma Kappa at Southern Illinois University and to all of my friends at the Laurel Springs Golf Club in Suwanee, Georgia.

I dedicate this book to the loving memory of my late mother Zenda Crone. I know how happy she would have been to have seen my success and my family. There was only one Zenda in this world, and I wish you all could have met her. She touched everyone she met like an angel from heaven.

Table of Contents

Introduction

I'm going to share with you some unique secrets that I use in my life that will hopefully help you become more successful, have a better attitude, make more money, and even become healthier. This isn't a book for the down and out; there are many books out there for them. This isn't a book about religion; this is a philosophical, no-nonsense approach to life. This book is targeted toward salespeople and executives who want to be more successful and reach their full potential in life and business. The bad news is, there are no silver bullets in life—there are no shortcuts. Before I depress you because there isn't a magic pill that you can take to instantly become a zillionaire, let me share one of the greatest secrets that I've learned in life, "a little bit over a long period of time." You are going to hear me say that over and over again. Hopefully, before long I'm going to turn on some switches in your head, and you are going to see the light of true success. Trust me; it really isn't that hard if you'll commit to making it happen and opening up your mind to new ideas and ways of thinking.

This book is truly how I live my life. This is from my heart. You might not agree with every theory, and that is OK. There is no one-size-fits-all shoe for success. Your shoe might be a little larger or smaller, maybe a different color. You need to get a little bit here and a little bit there. To find your perfect-fitting shoe, I'm hoping you will pick up a few ideas from this book. I learned my lessons from the school of hard knocks. I'm one of you, meaning that I paid the price, made the sales calls, went to work when I didn't want to, listened to idiot bosses when I didn't want to, and kept at it.

All business people who desire to be successful will at least appreciate (if not learn a few tricks from) my experiences. Whether you are just starting out or have been in the business world for some time, I hope that many of my secrets help you, "a little bit over a long period of time." For those of you who understand exactly what I'm talking about, I would love to hear any ideas that might expand upon my philosophies. The more we can share with those who want to learn, the more successful we all can be.

In 1993 I joined a small computer supply company. I helped build this company into a fast growing company. We sold the company in 1998. I've spent the past seven years living many people's dream—golfing almost every single day. Now, I've reached the point in my life where I've lived my dream of golfing my brains out. I'm ready to head into the next chapter of my life. I hope that chapter will be assisting many of you in reaching your potential.

So, how did I come up with "a little bit over a long period of time"? I'm the type of person who needs things simple. Even though I consider myself reasonably intelligent, I prefer things in black-and-white. I always say the "proof is in the pudding," which means that I really want to understand why things work the way they do and why people act the way they do. I'm only convinced things are the correct way when I've tried and failed and seen the proof for myself. I am by no means a psychologist, but I feel I am a philosopher of sorts.

During my younger years when I was running a million miles per hour, attempting to find the short cuts to success, I quickly learned that there really aren't any shortcuts in life. After I learned that I wasn't going to become a millionaire in a few months, I really started to find ways to achieve success the old-fashioned way.

To come up with some of my ideas, I studied nature and the way the world works. Often in my sales meetings, I would refer to the "tree theory." Look at that 125-year-old mighty oak. It started out as a little seedling and, relative to its size, grew rapidly during its first few years of existence. It would sprout some new branches each year, and over time it would grow into a huge, mighty oak, able to withstand storms and the dire conditions that life can often bring. It might lose a branch here or there, but it is so large and diversified that it can normally withstand any normal hit and keep on growing; and such is life.

If you are going to become a mighty oak, then you need to grow slowly—"a little bit over a long period of time." Then before you know it, your growth will be a hundredfold compared to your original starting point. You must understand nature and how things work and be patient. Just keep moving forward, and your tree will soon grow. Concentrate on those singles and doubles; your effort shouldn't be on hitting it out of the ballpark every time you are up to bat. Those homeruns will happen once in awhile but we can't predict them or count on them. It's the singles and doubles that will add up over time. In this book I will show you the many tips I've come up with that I use in my daily life that truly add up "a little bit over a long period of time."

I hope to change the way we all want something for nothing and the way we want everything overnight. It's great to press and push hard, but our expectations need to be guided toward the long-term and what we can control on a daily basis. Doing a little bit every single day of your life is how you can become healthy, rich, and successful. Finding what you should be doing everyday is what I'll discuss in this book.

I want you to read this book "a little bit over a long period of time," just how I wrote it. Sometimes it's hard for a busy salesperson or executive to allow a few hours to pour through a book, but we all have a few minutes every day. If you can read about a chapter a day, then you will have this book read in a week or so. If you can complete a few of the challenges I offer you, I can assure you that you will start heading down a path in your life you may never have thought was possible.

One example of "a little bit over a long period of time" is my piggy bank. I have saved change for most of my life, throwing loose change from my pockets into an empty fresh water container. It is this actual water container pictured on the front cover of this book.

On a side note, I have a twofold purpose for this little neurotic process of saving change. My plan is, when I reach the age of eighty or so, to break out my piggy bank and search for all of those old valuable coins that may be collectibles. Secondly, when I first started out with my career back in the early eighties, I actually lived off of my saved change when I was between jobs. I called this my hamburger fund. Even though at this point in my life I pray that I never need this loose change to eat on, I still have in the back of my mind how important this loose change was for me and how symbolic this change is in using my theory of "a little bit over a long period of time."

Now the water jug is almost full. So the point of this example is truly how "a little bit over a long period of time" can add up. Just by adding a few coins per week over the past twenty years or so the coins have really added up. This is how we need to view our lives, our health and our attitudes. Of course I'm not making any interest on this loose change, but it is amazing how quickly this jug of change has added up and is now like a mighty oak tree. See if you can find other ways to use this example in your own life. What things do you do that will add up "a little bit over a long period of time?" Look at the habits in your life, good or bad, and see what you can add or delete. It's those little things we do that will add up greatly over time.

There are many examples of how things can add up "a little bit over a long period of time." Hopefully, I can stimulate this thinking in your life so that you can see how this process can work. I also hope to help you understand the process of true success with either your career or your personal life.

I can relate this to many things we have to do in life. If you know your deadline, then break it up. Just do a little chunk of work each day and you will make your deadline with ease. Things really do add up. As a matter of fact I have written this book "a little bit over a long period of time." I committed to spending about fifteen to thirty minutes per morning working on my pre-written draft and before I knew it, with a little bit of effort each day, I had a book coming to life, and the effort felt pretty easy. Putting in just a small amount of effort each day, I was able to watch the pages add up over time.

Make sure you are doing things every day that will actually add up "a little bit over a long period of time." One example I used to tell my salespeople was to set a minimum number of sales calls to make per day. Make three cold calls per day, and you will have made fifteen in a week and 780 in a year. It will really add up if you just do "a little bit over a long period of time."

Most people need ways to deal with the issues in life. I have many interesting and unique philosophies I use that I want to share that will be able to help you, as well. Even though we all like the nice things that success brings, I'd like to change the way we think about "things" and the speed at which we expect to get them. Great things will come over time. Put the seeds in place, and we'll reap the harvest together—"a little bit over a long period of time." We need to concentrate on the process and not just the rewards. Remember that most rewards in life are a by-product of success, not success itself.

I'm a deep thinker. I always look at things we do in life and attempt to look deep inside and understand the meaning of not only *what* we are doing but *why* as well. I've spent most of my life trying to think about who we are, where we are going, and how are we going to get there. I certainly don't know all of the answers, but I'm confident that I'm heading down the right path. Where that path will lead nobody knows. All we can do is keep pushing forward, trying to make the best out of any situation we find ourselves in.

Some people feel our destiny is planned; others think we create it. My view of destiny is that there are some things in life we can control, some we can't. We just have to roll with the punches and try to control what we can and make the best out of what we can't.

I suppose one of the reasons I'm such a deep thinker is that I was adopted as a baby. For those of you out there who were adopted, you might know what I'm talking about. We often spend much time wondering where we came from, why we are here, and where we are going. Maybe being adopted is one of the reasons I have come up with so many of my philosophical ideas. As a side note, my wife was adopted as well, which I feel is pretty unique. I'm not trying to make any political statement here at all. If by chance some of my ideas work well for you, I would like you to know as much about the author as possible.

You can make changes *today* that will start moving your life in the right direction, and, before you know it, your momentum will take you to new levels that you may never have thought were possible. These changes will only start to happen if you decide to take action *today*, not tomorrow. I'll show you many different ways to think and act that should be able to get you started on the correct path. Once I get you started, it will all be up to you.

This is not a hand-holding book. You are going to have to work hard because, remember, nothing comes easy in life. If it did, then everyone would be equally successful. It takes just a small amount of effort each and every day that will really add up over time to make positive things happen in your life.

One of the greatest ways for any person or any company to become successful is to serve others. When we serve others we are providing a service which will help make businesses or people's life easier. It is my personal goal to assist salespeople and executives who are striving to reach their potential by providing you with some new and interesting ways to become more successful. I'm hoping during this journey that I can help many of you find your way and continue to add to my knowledge so that I can continue to grow and learn in this great process we call life.

I'm convinced that learning never stops. If learning ever does stop then you are either dying or going in the wrong direction. Our brains have the ability and capacity to continue learning for the majority of our lives. If we can just keep pushing forward, the answers to life will present themselves. Having the faith and belief that things will ultimately work out sustains us during our down times. It's easy to make it through the good times; it's how we handle the bad times that can separate us from the crowd and move us closer to our goals. We've heard this before, but I'll say it again. Never ever give up.

Chapter 1

Running to Something or Running from Something?

Most achievers in life gather their knowledge a little bit here and a little bit there. Some of the greatest influences in my life have been from books I have read. I've probably read almost every popular motivational book written. For a couple years, I spent almost every hour while driving in my car listening to motivational tapes. I belonged to a health club that had a mental gym, which back in the early nineties had almost every popular motivational tape ever made. These tapes were very important in shaping my belief system.

I have purposefully not read any motivational books over the past seven years or so. I have done this so that my writing would not be directly influenced by any one motivational book.

When it comes to motivation, the first thing I think of is a comment by the famous motivator Anthony Robbins. He says that we do most all things in life for one of two reasons. We are either seeking pleasure or avoiding pain. You can take almost any example in life and put it to the test with this logic. Ask yourself, "Am I doing this to gain pleasure or avoid pain?" Sometimes the answer to this question will be both to seek pleasure and avoid pain. Also, you might find that your answer to this question changes over time. For example, I've been a jogger for over twenty-five years now. When I first started jogging I wanted to get into shape at college after my first six months of overeating and not exercising. You might say that I was seeking pleasure by running and by the benefits I thought it might bring. I also wanted to avoid the pain I felt from gaining weight. Again, I only imagined that running would bring these benefits since I hadn't actually received the benefits yet. So I had to have a certain level of trust in my beliefs about the outcome of running. The bottom line is that we need to better understand why we do things, so that we can self-direct our motivation to better suit our needs and fulfill our goals. If we can understand whether we are seeking pleasure or avoiding pain then sometimes we can come up with a solution to our current situation. Spend some time thinking about the actions we are doing and then we can better understand what our ultimate goals are.

Now that I've been running for all of these years, I have to honestly say that I get out that door every morning because I'm afraid of not running and losing all those twenty-five years of running that I've put in. Now, you might say that I'm avoiding the pain by running because I know how much pain I would go through mentally if I was to become a non-runner.

What this example shows is how things can change even though we are doing the same thing. The mind is a tricky thing. We must understand its influences and motivations and put them in their proper place. Take examples in your life and apply the "seeking pleasure or avoiding pain" theory and figure out why you are doing the things you are doing.

One example might be overeating. Are you eating because you are hungry or are you eating because you are just trying to feel good? Once you figure out why you are doing a certain action, then you can start to find ways to either increase the positive actions or decrease the negative actions just by understanding your motivations.

Running for me now is like mowing the grass in my yard. If I don't mow, then my grass is going to get too long and not look good. I have to run regularly to keep myself in shape just like I have to mow regularly to keep my lawn in shape. Similarly, for me running is much like brushing my teeth in the morning. I could never imagine going a few days without brushing my teeth and that is exactly the way I want you to feel about running (or whatever exercise you choose) once you start building the habit of exercising.

After so many years of running regularly, I've reached the point where I don't feel that much different physically or mentally from the daily running I do. However, when I don't run or, God forbid, miss a couple days in a row, I can feel the degradation in my body and the declining process starting to affect my mind. To appreciate being out of shape, you must learn what it feels like to be in shape. If you've never been in shape, then you are going to have to just trust me on this. Being in good shape is the foundation for life; without good health our successes will mean nothing. If you finally get to a point in your career where you have financial success what good will it be if you are not in the best physical shape possible? There are certain things in life we can control and other things we can't control. Exercising and attempting to live a healthy life is certainly in our control. Our goal should be, to be in better shape at the age of 70 than we were as a young person.

Am I getting into any better physical shape now from running the same amount all of these years? Probably not, but I know that I'm keeping my weight at a good level and my heart and mind in shape. I also know that over time I'm still building up the stamina and dedication in my life for preserving and stimulating good health. I am also absolutely sure of what will happen to my mind and body if I don't exercise. I would get out of shape and I'm sure start to travel down a negative path in life, and that is something I certainly don't want to experience. I'm avoiding the pain by exercising and seeking pleasure by staying in shape.

The dedication I've built up with my running carries over to all other facets in my life. There are many chores at work and in life that we must do on a daily basis, and if you can develop the habit of exercising you can also build up many other similar habits in your daily life. Another important point is that you are going to be able to handle the stress and the work load much better than your competitors, who might not be in good physical and mental shape.

There is one question that often comes up when people are speaking of exercising: Does the mind have a greater effect on one's body or does the body have a greater effect on one's mind? You could argue it either way; however, they are certainly interrelated to some degree. Your mind has to have the ability to develop good exercising habits and the will and drive to create the motivation for a lifetime of exercising. But also, your healthy body can motivate your mind by giving you confidence, which can turn into a self-fulfilling prophecy that leads you to your goals. The better shape you get in, the better your body will look, the better your body looks, the better your mind will feel. This propels you to even greater levels of physical and mental fitness and success.

Another trick I want to share is that I have learned that if I run then certain things happen naturally in my life, almost as though I'm on cruise control. I know if I run, I will feel a certain way—positive, great, and full of ambition and hope for the future. You have to remember that aerobic exercise creates natural chemicals in your body and mind called endorphins that will make you feel better and more motivated.

I know that if I can just hit that door for my daily runs, the planets in my universe will be in alignment. I also know that if I don't run on any given day that for that particular day my mind will start to change rapidly and things will seem out of order to me. I will start to rationalize why I'm not running and often end up doing something negative, like breaking into the candy, or not doing something positive. I have found through the years that I'm so much more positive on the day and life if I can just hit that door and go for my run.

Let me give you two tips about running that you can use in whatever exercise you choose to do. First and foremost is that initially you should do much less exercising than you want to do. Understand that the mind and body are closely related and in order to train both of them, you have to train your mind first and your body second. Before you begin to exercise for the first time your body will not be hurting, and it will be fresh. You will feel great and want to train for an extended period. This is the danger area that I want you to be aware of. Because you aren't sore yet, you will think this new activity is easy, so you will over do it. If you over do it, you will become sore and in an attempt to avoid the pain, you will not exercise and a cycle will form.

Remember this is a lifestyle change we are talking about, not a fad, so we need to think in terms of doing this for the rest of our lives. The finish line is way out there so we need to take it easy and pace ourselves. Because life is "a little bit over a long period of time" we have to get our mind and our body in shape "a little bit over a long period of time." To train your mind you must feel as though your exercise is your way to that pot of gold, and you have to build up the habits of exercising.

Second, I have another blunt statement. If you don't plan to exercise for the rest of your life, then don't even bother. Maintaining excellent health is the mode we all want to eventually achieve. Like any fad in life, like a diet, if you don't make the change permanent then you won't maintain the desired results. Twenty-five years ago, it took me about six months to get my body into reasonably good health. I've maintained that good health for all of these years, but it would probably only take about three short months of not exercising for my body to revert back to the unhealthy state it was in when I started, not to mention what it would do to my mind. The point I want to make is that I could literally throw away twenty-five years of hard work in just a few months; that alone is motivation enough to keep me jogging for the rest of my life.

I can't stress enough that your goal needs to be to create a new lifestyle that will last the rest of your life. I have nothing against someone who wants to go out and exercise once in awhile just for fun, but if you truly want to achieve the life lasting benefits of exercising, then exercising has to be just as important in your life as eating food and drinking water. How would you fair if you quit eating and drinking water the rest of your life? That is how I want you to feel about exercising. Those benefits are sitting right in front of you. All you have to do is take the first step—"a little bit over a long period of time." It's not that hard. If I can do it, you can do it, too. If you have tried and failed in the past then I ask you to please give my exercising ideas a try. These ideas just might work and help change your life.

To exercise for the long-term you must find a time that is a set schedule and cannot be changed much. When I was in college, I ran around four in the afternoon before dark and before dinner. Once I hit the working world, I found the only time I could routinely and consistently run was to run early in the morning at sunrise and before work. This was because there were too many work issues or social engagements that came up after work that would get in the way of my working out.

Now that I'm my own boss, I choose to run at 9:00 AM and to be home before the 9:30 AM open on Wall Street. Wall Street isn't going to wait for me so I have an extra incentive to hit that door. Whatever time you choose it must be fairly consistent and be one of the most important times of your day. Remember, if you want the planets in your life aligned, you must give them a constant orbit from which to work.

Not having enough time is not a good enough excuse for not exercising. If you don't have enough time to allow for thirty minutes of exercise five days per week, then you need to reconsider your priorities. We all find time to watch a bit of TV, have a snack, or do little wasteful things here or there. Exercising will have to become one of the major focal points in your life, and the rest of your daily life will need to revolve around "your" workout time. One of the reasons I gravitated towards running in the morning was so that I could get it done and over with. It was just too easy at times to come up with excuses as the day wore on to not exercise. If you can, make exercising one of the first things you do to start your day—after your first cup of coffee, of course.

For years I used to keep a record of my workouts. At first I used a diary to list my times and how I felt. This was important because it gave me a record of my progress. It also gave me an incentive to not miss a day, because I would have to visually be reminded that I didn't work out. As time went on I began to use a monthly calendar that was near my shower and posted for the rest of my family to view. This provided a visual reminder of my running. Most importantly, when I had a day or two when I couldn't work out I would put a big X on that date. I hated to put those X's on my calendar, and it gave me even more incentive to get out that door so I could post my time on my calendar and make it a good week or a good month. Because I had my running calendar posted on the wall of my bathroom I regularly had time to stare at my running calendar and monitor my progress. Putting this calendar up was a great motivational tool for me, and I suggest to anyone who is new to working out to use this tool as an incentive to keep you on track.

I use running as my example, but there are many exercises that people could do for the rest of their lives. I chose running because it was something that was only dependent on me and the weather. I don't have to depend on others or equipment. All I need are some shorts, a pair of good running shoes, a pair of Thorlo running socks, and a road.

This is one of the most important points on exercising: *exercise much less than you want to.* I will repeat this many times in this book but you have to trust me on this. After twenty-five years of jogging, I'm still only jogging around thirty minutes per day. Several times I have run a half a marathon and feel as though I probably could run a whole marathon, but that is not the point. I love running, not because I love to run, but because I love the benefits that are gained through my running. If you are going to run for the rest of your life you must get in shape mentally. Again I wish I could look you in the eyes when I say this: *for the first three months of your new exercise program only run ten minutes per day and not a minute more.*

Since we want to plan on exercising for the rest of our lives, we don't want to damage our bodies from overuse. I know that at some point in my life I may need to switch to another exercise. If that time comes, I'll probably switch to swimming. For now, I plan on jogging for the rest of my life, "a little bit over a long period of time."

It is more important to build up the habit and train your mind for working out than it is to change your body quickly. If you try to change your body quickly, it will break down. This will make it easy for your mind to justify being lazy, and it will make excuses for you to not exercise in order to avoid the pain.

If you can train your mind to just get you out that door and realize how good you are going to feel once you are done, after three months you will have achieved the mental stamina and habit to start increasing your time up to that magical thirty minutes at which you can achieve aerobic fitness. This is the mental fitness that will start to align your planets.

Once you hit three months then it is OK to start adding one minute or so a month until you reach the level you desire. You may find you have the time and energy to run or work out for forty-five or sixty minutes, but I would never suggest going over those amounts. If you overtrain your body will ultimately breakdown and you will fail. Remember, we are attempting to maintain these results for the rest of our lives, so let's not be in a huge hurry to get to that finish line. It is the number of years you exercise for the rest of your life that will count, not how much you can run tomorrow. We'll get to that finish line "a little bit over a long period of time."

After many years of running, my mind is actually to the point that on days when I don't feel like running, I do one of two things. I either do a three-quarter-length run just to take it a bit easy as I'm listening to what my body is telling me, or once in a blue moon I just might take the day off if my body is telling me that I shouldn't go jogging.

After all these years of running, I've learned that when I'm finished with my run, I'm going to feel much better than when I started out for my run. I'm actually more motivated to hit the road if I don't feel that great before it's time to run because I've learned that I'm going to feel great when I'm done, I'm seeking pleasure. Maybe this is the true relativity theory. Conversely speaking, at times when I feel great before I run I sometimes have my worst runs, perhaps because I run a bit too hard and my expectations are set too high.

I can't stress enough that almost all of the positive thoughts and influences in my life have come about from my great physical health. Many of my inspirations have come during my runs when I have just myself and my mind to listen to. If you want to change your life and be the best you can be, don't wait; start today. Go out there and give me ten minutes five days a week or every other day for the next month.

Since this isn't a book just about running, I want to end this section on running with this reminder: if you want to get better, achieve your full potential, make more money, feel better, and look better, then you have to either get into shape or maintain the great shape that you might already be in.

Ask yourself this: do you want to change your life? I want you to trust me with this. Make the commitment—no matter what—to set your mind to it and start implementing my exercise program for the next month. It will be easy if you just do "a little bit over a long period of time."

Tips for Running

When you run, run away from your home as opposed to running around the block or back and forth near your house. If you run away from your home, in a sense you will only have to run half of the distance because once you are away from your home, you will be motivated to run back to it. This feeling must come from the caveman or pack theory of safety and survival. I've often encountered this feeling when I'm traveling away from home. I'll take a stop watch with me, and if I'm going out for a forty- minute jog, which I normally do on vacation, I feel as though I only have to run twenty minutes. Then I turn around and don't even have to look at my watch, and the time, for some reason, seems much shorter. I can also just relax and enjoy my run versus concentrating on where I'm going. Try it.

Have a special pair of quality running shoes that you only wear for running, no matter how cool they may look. Buy the best pair of running shoes you can afford. For most of my running career, I've had good luck with Nike.

Always wear great socks when running. I have never found any socks better than Thorlo socks. An investment in these quality socks will pay dividends in comfort and preventing injury.

Run the same route for a year or two at a time. Then you don't have to wear a watch and you can just let your mind relax and enjoy the run instead of wondering where or how far you may be running. I actually run the same route for about five years at a time.

Work on affirmations a few times during your run. Find a tree or a lamppost a few hundred yards ahead of you and focus on saying your affirmations until you pass the point you were focusing on. (For those who don't know, affirmations are small thoughts or sayings that you will repeat over and over again to stimulate your motivation. Affirmations I've used in the past are, "I feel great", "I will make things happen", "I will have a great attitude". You can come up with your own affirmations that fit your particular goals.)

Work on your breathing; make sure you take deep breaths with good rhythm and occasionally take a deep breath stretching your rib cage fully. When I'm at my typical jogging pace I normally take three steps for each breath in and out.

Don't be afraid to spit when needed. This is your body's way of getting rid of toxins. Along with sweating, spitting is one of the best ways to cleanse your system. I also love to clear my nasal passages after about a half mile into my run. You definitely want to get that mucous out of you because your body will be trying to cleanse itself as it tries to get into shape.

Keep a good pair of sunglasses handy, if you are running in the sun. You don't want to add stress to your run by having to strain your eyes for thirty minutes or more.

Stretch after you run, but not much before. Your muscles will be warmed up, ready, and supple after you have finished running. Have a routine, and do the same stretches after every run. Take at least a few minutes stretching. I do a bit of yoga after my runs. At the age of forty-three, I can still easily touch my toes. Losing flexibility is one of the negative side effects of aging. Stay flexible and you will feel and act younger. I plan on stretching after every run for the rest of my life. This should really add up "a little bit over a long period of time."

Try to run in quiet places if possible. I run through my neighborhood, which is quiet and large. Personally, I don't like to run with friends or other runners, as I prefer to run at my own pace and keep my mind open for thinking. When it is quiet during my run I often have my best inspirations.

In this game of trying to get ahead in life it is important to remember on those cold and rainy days when you don't feel like stepping out in the horrible weather that if you do go running, you are truly separating yourself from the pack. If you can run on bad days, then think how easy it will be to run on a beautiful day. However, never run through lightning storms, of course.

Some of my most memorable runs have come through bad weather and rainstorms. It is hard to explain, but I feel there is a connection to God and nature when running through a rain- or snowstorm. Assuming I have the proper rain gear or warm clothing, I have always had a sense of being one with nature during those runs in inclement weather. I remember once in Florida a guy approached me during a rain storm and asked if I was actually jogging. He was afraid I needed some help or something, or maybe he just thought I was nuts because it was raining so hard.

If possible, try to run at the same time every day. If you have a set time you will be pushed out that door. If you know you have to leave for work by 7:00 AM then you know you will have to start your run no later than 6:00 AM or so. Having a deadline to run is the best way to keep yourself motivated and on schedule. For fifteen years I ran every day at 6:00 AM. It wasn't easy, but boy did I feel great once I started the working day. I had already accomplished more by 8:00 AM than most people would have accomplished in an entire day.

It's OK once in a blue moon to miss a day. Matter of fact, once every few weeks or so missing a day of working out can motivate you further because you realize what you miss. But be careful to consider your mental and physical state and gauge whether a day off will do you more good than harm. Like everything in life, moderation is the key. In this case we want moderation to be those few days that we don't exercise.

Some people might be concerned about dogs. I run in a nice neighborhood, and 99 percent of the time nice neighborhoods produce nice dogs. They may sound a bit mean, but normally these doges aren't trying to kill you. They are just protecting their territory. In my twenty-five years of running I have found that if I am bigger than the dog, I will normally show him who is boss and almost always they will run away with their tails between their legs. There have been a few instances when I knew I would be up for a hard fight. I pulled the friendly approach, stopping my run, putting my hand out, palms down, and showing Fido that I wanted peace.

In one instance recently, I had a rather large, overweight bulldog charge me, and I just simply out ran him. For those of you who don't run in nice neighborhoods, I suggest extreme caution as most dogs will mimic their owner's personality. Carrying a can of mace or pepper spray may not be a bad idea. With that said, I can assure you that if I were in an area where I couldn't find peace with my runs, then I would move to another area or fix the problem, since running is such an important part of my life. You must have peace on your run so you can enjoy the experience.

I have the same exact routine after every run. I stretch for a bit, and then I get a big glass of water and 1000 mg of vitamin C. I may get about one cold per year, but I'm convinced that with exercise, proper sleep, and a good attitude, vitamin C will be the only medicine I will need for the rest of my life. I know we can all get sick with diseases, and there are situations that are out of our control. I just want to attempt to control the sicknesses I can. Keeping your immune system strong is one of the most important aspects for a healthy life. While working at my last company, I may have missed half a day of work because of not feeling well. This was over a seven-year period.

Lastly, I want to leave this message loud and clear. If you believe the benefits of exercising regularly can change your life and help assist you in reaching your potential, please remember that you are going to need to exercise for the rest of your life. In order to achieve that goal you will have to begin slowly if you are currently not in shape, physically or mentally. Achieving material success will mean nothing if you are not healthy. Start aligning your planets each day for the rest of your life and get in shape.

10K Races

Over my twenty-five-year jogging career I've run many 10K races. Lately I haven't run them because of Saturday morning golf and having a family, but in the first fifteen years of my running career, I did run many 10K races, probably one hundred or so. My fastest time was somewhere around forty minutes, which isn't too bad compared to most runners. However, forty minutes will never get you into the Olympics. The Olympic runners are running some-where well below the thirty-minute level. They are running, not jogging.

The point of this section is just to pass along my wisdom of running 10K races and to explain how I had a blast passing over half of the field. In most of these 10K races most of the runners are new to the game of jogging and racing. A large portion of the field, excluding the elite runners, sprint off of the starting line and attempt to run to the front of the pack. This is easy for about half a mile or so, until they realize they are running at about a six-minute-mile pace, and then reality hits. I've made this mistake before, and nothing is more embarrassing than either having to stop, because you were going too fast, or having most of the field pass you as you feel you are dying from exhaustion.

I learned that the secret for these races is much like my theory in this book, "a little bit over a long period of time." Of course this is the classic rabbit and hare story, but nonetheless it holds true in racing and in life. It is so fun for me to just hold back and enjoy my little jog at the beginning of the race and watch all these people clamoring to try to pass me. I love to see who these people are, as I know they are going to be my victims later in the race. Some of them are much like rush-hour drivers—very impatient and rude as they hurriedly attempt to pass and to squeeze through the crowd.

Near mile one I start picking off my victims. I've been jogging comfortably all this time, running somewhere between a 7.5- and 8.5-minute mile at the beginning, and then I start to pick up my pace. Remember, at this pace we aren't going to be running a sub-forty-minute race. At the age of forty-three, that is no longer my goal. I want to enjoy things and run "my" race. Over the next few miles I'll start to pass about a quarter of the field, those who started out too fast and are laboring like they are going to die. Somewhere around mile four or five, when I'm comfortably cruising at my seven-minute pace, I really come on strong, silently gaining on the rest of the field. This is just like life. People are always trying to find the easy way out or attempting to run to the front of the line; but when the race gets tough (like life) they aren't in a position to keep getting stronger until the finish. This is the philosophy I want you to learn when it comes to business and your personal life.

You don't have to win the race or be first in life to be a winner. Running my 10K races was a bit like using my potential. You have to keep moving forward and getting stronger. Near the end of the race I would end up running with people who were pretty good runners and would even notice a few who had the same strategy as myself. Ironically there would be a few of the front runner sprinters who managed to hang on throughout the race because they either were stupid or really do have some hidden potential even though they weren't in shape. These people probably weren't able to walk the next day, and their mind certainly wasn't going to want them to come back and feel that pain again.

So the moral of this story is don't run to the front of the pack, even though it is hard to hold back. Sometimes it is smarter to just lie back a bit, whether in running or in life, and then start making your move. Run within yourself and finish at a strong and forceful pace. This attitude will help you "seek the pleasure" of running (and life) and put you near the front of the pack, separating you from the rest of the herd. Separating yourself from the rest of the herd is truly how you get ahead in the business world.

Stock Car Drafting Theory

One of the hardest things for most people to do, when it comes to exercising, is to find a convenient time to work out. I've come up with a magical formula that works for me. It allows me to fit in daily exercises such as sit-ups, pushups, arm curls, and so forth. Let me share it with you. I call this drafting because much like in stock car races, when a car follows another car closely, they actually can go faster with less power; thereby conserving their fuel and increasing their horsepower when they want to pass.

While I was in college, I started using the drafting theory without even realizing it. When I used to take a shower in my fraternity I started doing pull-ups on the bathroom stalls. I would do these pull-ups every time I took a shower and began to feel guilty if I didn't do my pull-ups first. The more I thought about this, after I got out of college and didn't have the bathroom stalls to hang from when doing to my pull-ups, the more I realized that I was drafting.

So what do you do on a regular basis in your life, during which you could throw in some quick exercises? For me it was turning on the shower in my house. My shower takes about two minutes to warm up, so I use this as the perfect opportunity to use my little sit-up machine and do forty-three sit-ups. (I do one for each year of my life and increase one per year). Forty-three sit-ups may not sound like much work and really isn't much work, but without really even trying I'm doing 215 sit-ups per week and 11,180 per year. I also do forty-three push-ups after I do my sit-ups. I've developed a habit of doing these exercises to kill the time while the shower is warming up, and what a wonderful opportunity to throw in those little pesky exercises which really do a huge benefit to your body and really add up "a little bit over a long period of time."

I take a shower every single day of my life, so I'm assured of doing my little workout now for the rest of my life. Do this for thirty days and you will develop the habit and you won't even have to think about dropping to the floor to get your exercises done.

Think about this theory and either implement my strategy of hitting the floor and spending about three minutes per work day or find something similar in your life that is very repetitive everyday so you can do some drafting of your own. Adding one push-up and sit-up per year isn't much, of course, but by the time I'm sixty-five I should still be in pretty good shape. Honestly I know that I'll hit a limit at some point in my life and will maybe even back off a few reps because the key is not to overdue it. Just get a little burn and you know the rest; do "a little bit over a long period of time."

You can always do more sit-ups and push-ups anytime during the day, but if you can do them before you step into the shower, I can assure you that in a few months you will notice the difference. More importantly, you will never need to join a gym, unless you really want to.

Action Items to Do Immediately

- Start today doing some type of ten-minute exercise (not a minute more). Wear a watch or have a clock nearby. Do this for one month and then start adding one minute per week until you reach between thirty and forty-five minutes.
- Post a calendar and mark the days you will exercise—every other day or Monday through Friday.
- Do five minutes of light stretching after your workout.
- Think of a positive affirmation to say a few times while exercising.
- Do 10 pushups and 10 sit ups while your shower is warming up. Add 1 per month until you reach 40 to 50. Make this part of your daily routine.

Chapter 2

Motivation

I've spent most of my life being philosophical. I'm a thinker and have always thought about the smartest and the shortest way to get from point A to point B. A bit ironic I suppose when the final answer has been "a little bit over a long period of time." However, I had to eliminate all other possibilities from the equation to come up with that answer for myself. To some degree I've never been able to take advice or direction from others; I always had to learn it on my own or make the mistake myself.

After I spent much time trying to work on my motivation I got down to the root of the problem; it is all a matter of time. For most people, if they think they have time left they aren't motivated. Most people are procrastinators who only do things just before it's too late.

The other significant point I came up with besides the importance of time was the gravity of the action we need to take. I have ended up doing some of my best work on a deadline. This pressure might not suit you, but I feel a rush of adrenaline when I am a bit anxious to meet an important deadline. My personality is such that I already know that I can perform; I just need the motivation to fully complete the task at hand. I almost enjoy the rush of trying to complete the project on time when time is starting to run out. There is a fine line between not having enough time to finish a project and having that adrenaline rush needed to feel the urgency of the situation.

Does It Really Matter?

Here is another good example I use to keep situations in perspective and to help my motivation. We have all been told that the world is around four and a half to five billion years old. Our life normally spans some seventy- to ninety-plus years. Comparing our lifespan to the length of the earth's lifespan puts things into perspective for me. Whatever the issue you are working on or worrying about, use this logic to put yourself at ease.

If you had a timeline of the Earth's nearly five billion years on a sheet of paper, starting from age zero to the current year of five billion, and then put your life span on that same graph, you wouldn't even be able to see your seventy to ninety years of life. I don't at all mean to say that our lives are insignificant. I just want to put into perspective that, in the big scheme of things, it "really doesn't matter." And someday in the future it really isn't going to matter to anyone or anything. In another few hundred years or even a thousand years, I don't think that anyone will realize or care about the action you are worrying about to the highest degree at this very moment.

Negative thinkers would take this logic and say why should we do anything right or responsible because it really doesn't matter. No one in the future will care. However, positive thinkers would take this same logic and have no fear. They would be able to separate their subconscious fears from the reality of living their dreams and break through the barriers of doubt. They will have the motivation to achieve all their goals and potential in life. They will also be able to put important projects and details that they are worrying about into proper perspective. When it comes down to it, only a few things really matter in life, that you love your family and that you positively affect as many people as you can during your lifetime. Anything else is just material and can probably be replaced.

Use time to assist you with your motivation. The other side of the timeline theory is the deadline theory. We have all had deadlines for which there would be serious consequences for not meeting them. One deadline I have always used is for my running as stated in the previous chapter. I really want to see the opening bell on Wall Street, and I have as yet ever seen them hold the bell for me if I was late for my run. It is truly amazing to me how I am literally pushed out of the door knowing the I have to be back by a certain time or I will face the consequence of missing the opening bell on Wall Street.

Find deadlines in your life that you can use as motivation and always find a way to beat the deadline. Don't be late, be on time. If possible break up your tasks into little parts. If you have a week until your deadline then break up your task into 7 parts and the effort will add up daily if you just commit to doing each little task.

When I ran the sales meetings for my company, I used to use perverse logic for the ultimate motivation. I want to preface this section as totally 100 percent hypothetical and only used as an example of how, at the extreme, humans can be motivated.

All salespeople have different levels of expertise and success. Why are some salespeople more motivated to make more sales calls and follow up than other salespeople? There are many different answers to that question. The point I want to make is that I could take almost any average salesperson and make them a top salesperson within a few days. I could take their motivation levels from a low point to the highest point in a matter of minutes. How could this be done? In a sick world we could all hold a gun to the head of our salespeople to make them make calls or get those orders "or else." Now once again I want to say this logic is a bit perverse and is only a joke to provide an example to show that our motivation levels can easily and truly be changed overnight. Although this is an exaggerated example, it demonstrates that there is a potential for change in all of us. If we can all believe that motivation can be changed, and if we are truly attempting to be more successful, attempting to live up to our full potential, then we are going to find the answers to self-motivation because we can *believe* that it is possible.

The ultimate answer, in my book, to cure your motivation needs is just to eliminate or reduce your tendency for procrastination. Just start the project, get the ball rolling, and, before you know it, you will be on your way. Do it now. Give yourself a deadline, and start doing a little bit of your project every day—"a little bit over a long period of time."

Do It Now!

Procrastination is one of the ball and chains of success. It is very normal to procrastinate because we think we are avoiding the pain of the project. I've often found myself screaming "do it now." Of course we all need to prioritize our projects, but I'm convinced that procrastinating has one major negative influence. It totally clutters our minds with projects or tasks that we know we need to do and clogs our system from creating new ideas. It's a bit like sticks and trash clogging a stream, not allowing the water to flow. We have to keep the clutter picked up from our minds so that the new ideas can flow freely. It is hard to move onto future projects if we are bogged down by the many unfinished projects in our mind.

Get in the habit of "do it now," and clear your list of those mindless little tasks. If needed, write them down and cross them off one by one. Keep reminding yourself that as soon as you get rid of those tasks your million-dollar idea will be flowing down the stream. The great side effect from this attitude is that if the idea does flow into your head you will already be in the habit of taking action and "doing it now."

Nothing's Easy

You've heard the saying: nothing good comes easy. I've added: if it was easy, then everyone would be doing it and it wouldn't be special anyway. If everyone in the world were rich then nobody would be rich, if you think about it. We would all be the same.

You have to train your mind to think that nothing comes easy. The only way to appreciate it, once you get it, is to work hard for it or maybe to lose it and get it back later. Then you'll learn to appreciate it.

One of the keys in life is to try to appreciate things without losing them, whether it is a material thing or maybe even your spouse or family. I almost get a bit nervous if something good comes too easy. We take them when they come, but the key is to remember to appreciate them if they do land in your lap. I believe this is one of the secrets of life.

I have been in the position to appreciate things when it comes to my personal situation. Even though I haven't had a "real" job in seven years, I still appreciate it in the morning when I hear the traffic report on the radio and hear how miserable traffic is during rush hour in Atlanta. But, like anything, you can have too much of a good thing. That is why I want to give back by writing this book and giving presentations to up-and-coming salespeople and managers. I honestly think I can stimulate some old-fashioned thinking and help get many future superstars on the correct path more quickly than they would have done on their own. Believe it or not, now I appreciate the act of going back to work.

You need to train your mind to believe that the hard work is part of the process. I say many times in this book, hard work is something that will separate you from most of the crowd. You need to trick your mind into thinking that the hard work is fun. If you really want to reach your goals, then put yourself into a mode in which nothing will get in your way. Hard work is not an obstacle, but rather something good that is part of the formula. Make hard work fun; it is seeking pleasure as it relates to your future success.

How Much Time Is Left?

Lord only knows how much time we have left on this earth. If we all knew the answer to that, I'm sure many of us would change what we are doing and how quickly we are doing it.

I like to pretend that our life is like a basketball game. There is a scoreboard up in the air that is showing our time clock. This clock is ticking down as we speak. It has some amount of time on it, but that amount for those of us who are healthy is an unknown. We might know what our average life expectancy is, but we don't know the unknown. We don't know if there are thirty-two minutes left or thirty-two years left. I don't bring up this notion to freak anyone out. I just point this out to remind all of us that there is only a certain amount of time we have left in our lifetime.

Just knowing that the clock is running down can, at times, give us motivation. It is much like a basketball team who knows they only have a few minutes left to come from behind. Often they are motivated to do some extraordinary actions. It also helps me put time and life in perspective to remember that our time here on earth won't last forever.

So think about your time clock up in the air. How much time is on your clock and can you actually put some time back on the clock by getting in better shape, eating better, and thinking better?

Think about your time running down, and see if it doesn't help get you off your butt and make some things happen, today. That buzzer is going to go off; just try to accomplish what you can before your time runs out. My goal is to try to live my life without any regrets, which is one of the reasons I got off my butt and got this book finished. Don't live your life with any regrets. Write down what you would want to do if you knew you only had a couple of years left in your life, and then do them so you won't have any regrets.

Action Items to Do Immediately

- Make a list of all the projects you need to get done, and do them now.
- Make a timeline on a sheet of paper showing the earth's age of around five billion years. Now mark your life expectancy of around eighty-five years to scale to put your life in perspective and quit worrying about so much.
- Visualize your scoreboard. See the clock ticking down? How much time do you have left? Use this motivation to do something that you have meant to do for years. Live your life without any regrets.

Chapter 3

Positive Thinking

The phrase positive thinking is overdone and overused. When I go out speaking, I do not want to be known as just a positive thinker or a motivational thinker. Many people get the wrong idea, thinking of a cheerleader and a person who is "up" all the time and, to a degree, is a bit unrealistic. I would prefer to be considered a philosophical, motivational, positive thinker.

My philosophy on positive thinking is more geared to turning situations to one's advantage. The true key ingredient involved with this process is keeping control of your attitude. I truly believe that if you lose control of your attitude, you have lost the battle. Keeping control of your attitude really means to remain calm, or at least attempt to remain calm, like the captain of a ship on rough seas. It takes work to control your attitude. You have to train your mind that hard work is one of the key ingredients necessary to separate yourself from all the other people in the world, who will not be in control of their attitudes and will do something stupid that will undermine their success.

It is easy and natural for most people to react with an angry or negative attitude to bad situations. Losing it and doing something stupid is the path of least resistance for the herd of people you are competing against. The people who are going to get ahead in this world are the ones who work to control their attitudes and turn most any situation into something positive, or at least not turn it into something negative. Take it from me, I used to have a serious problem controlling my attitude; I had to learn from my mistakes or keep facing the consequences.

You can almost make it a game in life to try to turn most any situation into something positive. Now, I always put disclaimers into everything I say because there are always exceptions to the rule, such as disasters and personal family tragedies. I'm not speaking about those few horrible incidents because I put those into different categories. Of course, we can turn some of those unfortunate situations into positives, too, but that endeavor would require a more religious slant than that of this book.

The situations I'm speaking about are those normal, everyday situations that happen in life, those mundane, "a little bit over a long period of time" things that happen to all of us. It is when these normal situations arise that you need to rise above the situation at hand, look at it from outside your natural reflexive emotions, and keep your cool. Either find a way to avoid the situation or find a calm way to turn the situation at hand to your advantage. Just staying calm and doing nothing, might win you the battle, since the people on the other side of the conflict will probably do something idiotic that will come back and haunt them over time.

I have found that one of the keys for me in controlling my attitude, when I find myself in a situation, in which people are losing control of their attitude or being real jerks about something, is to say to myself "keep control of your attitude." This really helps, and I almost get a smile on my face because I know that I'm on the correct path since I'm aware of my attitude. Most people lose control of their attitude without even realizing it. One of the messages that I would love to get across in this book is that we need to be aware of our actions before we do something stupid. For those of us hard chargers in life, we will always find ourselves in situations that are getting out of control because we normally are attempting to make things happen. This means that someone on the other end will probably have to do some more work and be unhappy about it.

The Brenda Theory

The company I helped run employed a woman whose life was out of control. Her name wasn't Brenda, but I'll use that name in this book so as not to persecute someone in public. Brenda was always late for work, always late paying bills, and always having "stuff" happen to her that made her life out of control. Over the period of a couple of years, I came to the conclusion that 99 percent of the stuff that happened to her was of her own making. In her mind she was never to blame for anything; she believed that this "bad stuff" would just come her way. She spent most of her time fixing problems and complaining about how bad things were, just about as negative as I can describe in print.

Sometimes Brenda would be late for work because she forgot to set her alarm. A few times, she was even later for work because she got a speeding ticket or got into a fender bender on her way to work because she was hurrying frantically to get to work on time. Once she got into an accident because she turned left across traffic and failed to put on her turn signal to let the cars behind her know where she was going. You can see where I'm going with this. She blamed "things" for her problems. If we analyze what was really going on, she was responsible for 99 percent of her own problems.

Sometimes she was late paying her car payments, so she would spend an additional twenty dollars, which she didn't have, to overnight her car payment. She never changed the oil in her car. One day her engine seized up because it was almost out of oil. She often got sick with colds and was not able to work. She was, of course, getting sick all of the time because she worried about everything and didn't take care of herself so her immune system was at a very low level.

What is the point of the Brenda theory? In almost all situations in life we are in control of our own situations. Brenda could have easily gotten up a few minutes earlier or insured her alarm was set each night so that she didn't have to speed to work. She could have been proactive turning on her turn signals and getting the oil changed on her car. Brenda was only reactive. I want you all to consider whether you are being proactive or reactive in your daily tasks.

We can't spend our time in life blaming others for our problems. Some problems will happen to us, but the winners in life learn from their mistakes and are proactive enough to prevent many problems from happening in the first place.

Just like controlling our attitude, we need to spend most of our time thinking about cause and effect in our life. We have to take control and realize that we are responsible for all of our actions. Blaming others or "life" is just a loser's mentality. If we spend most of our time fixing problems that we could have prevented, we will never get ahead. We aren't using our minds for positive thinking, we need to be proactive in life, not reactive, if we want to help shape our futures for the better.

Don't be a Brenda. Remind yourself of the Brenda theory and get your act together. Take 100 percent of the responsibility for everything in your life and blame no one but yourself for anything you do. Your actions are the one thing that you truly have control over in life.

Most people normally react negatively to situations that don't fit their views. This is normal and is exactly the reason we must train ourselves not to react to situations with anger. Anger will cause us to do something stupid that we will probably regret later when we've settled down.

Remember, one of the keys in life is being able to do something that is hard; it separates us from the masses. Trust me when I say the masses are negative, reactionary thinkers taking paths of least resistance.

Take a drive in rush hour and notice the responses of the average person who gets cut off in traffic or who appears to be running late and in a hurry. They really act like idiots, honking their horns, giving people the finger, and other obnoxious behaviors. They are reacting so negatively to a situation that they really have no control over. And their negative reactions will have no beneficial effect on their futures. In fact, they could get shot and killed by some angry stranger they offend. My point here is not to talk about rush hour traffic, but to point out how most of the world reacts negatively to stress, and how they aren't in control of their attitudes.

It's not that negative things don't happen; it's just that reacting to them like an idiot isn't going to improve anything. When you think about it, you have a choice about how you react to anything. If we really want to live happy stress-free lives then all we can really do is remain calm and figure out a positive spin on the situation. I have a thousand examples of times in my life when negatives things happened to me, yet I found ways to turn them into positive things.

One example dates back about twenty years ago. My partner and I owned a computer company and were cash strapped. We had a small line of credit with the bank, and, for some reason, the bank screwed up our balance and bounced one of our checks to a vendor. Being a new company we were very concerned about the appearance of our cash position, so this put us into a very uncomfortable situation.

There were a number of ways we could have reacted to this problem. We could have called up the bank and ranted and raved about how our business was damaged by the bank's inept actions. Instead we called up the bank manager and asked for a lunch date. We calmly sold ourselves, our company, and the exciting story we had for our vision. We politely explained the situation and detailed the potential future damage this unfortunate situation could cause to our future relationships with our vendors.

To make a long story short, the banker was so impressed with our story and situation that he not only called our vendor and apologized on our behalf, but also gave us a line of credit more than ten times larger than we previously had. So again, take this example and put into the equation the typical ranting and raving that a customer like Brenda would do, and then imagine the end result. The bank would probably have found a way to get rid of our business if we had acted like mad idiots over the situation.

Furthermore, if I couldn't have resolved the situation to my satisfaction, I have another rule in life. Avoid negative people and situations. I would have simply ended my relationship with my bank (calmly) and found a new relationship with a bank that hopefully would meet my future needs.

Gravitate towards your goals and avoid negative people and situations. Things have a way of working out. Maybe it is the natural order in the world, but I'm convinced that you will attract friends and business associates who have similar views as you do.

When I ran my company, I was known for saying, "We never have problems, only opportunities." After awhile it was interesting to see the reactions of most of my positive-thinking employees. For instance, they might come up to me with smirks on their faces and say, "Boy, we have a great opportunity; our largest customer is furious with us because their product didn't arrive on time." We all make mistakes, even the best performers. It is how we handle these mistakes that separates us from our competition.

I learned early on in business that there are many crooks, cheaters, and liars out there. This made me realize that it really wasn't that hard to succeed in business, if you were just an honest businessman.

The easiest way to separate yourself from most of the working world is to simply tell the truth. Even if the truth isn't exactly good news, your customer will appreciate it in the long run because they will know you are a person of integrity. If your customer doesn't appreciate the truth, and assuming you aren't making that many mistakes, then you really may not want that client as a customer anyway.

You can make a game out of trying to make something positive out of something that has gone wrong. In reality if other people make mistakes and they are good people, then you have leverage in the situation to turn the table and make something good out of it. Keep your cool and don't think emotionally, think rationally.

Surround Yourself with Positive People

This may sound obvious, but surrounding yourself with positive people will help propel you faster to your goals. With that said, I'd like to make an important observation from my viewpoint. You can't convert negative-thinking people into positive-thinking people unless they want to change for themselves.

It is hard to stay positive and have a good attitude when things are not going well. It is because it is hard, you can separate yourself from the negative people who are going nowhere fast. Negative people are taking the path of least resistance by being negative and having a bad attitude. They are taking the easy way out.

Converting negative thinkers is a bit like watching crossfire on CNN and having each party agree with the other's viewpoint; it isn't going to happen. I've tried to convert negative thinkers, and all I do is get frustrated by them puking out complaints about how bad the world is and how everyone else is to blame. Remember, we captain our own ship, and if the waters are rough, then we need to change course and move in another direction until we reach our goals.

We have to have the belief that "we will find a way" no matter what. Negative people will give up, but positive people will find a solution, one way or another. We may not know the answer immediately, but we have to believe that the answer will come, as it always does if we just hang in there and keep pushing forward.

All you can do is maintain your positive attitude and put out your force field to repel people's negative attitudes. Ignore them when they complain about problems (problems they probably created themselves), say that nothing will get better, or say that you just can't do it.

If you ask these negative thinkers why, they will just say

"because." You will naturally repel these people over time, as they will feel bummed out that they can't bring you down to their level so you can commiserate with them about how bad the company is being run or about that crummy boss you all have. People who spend most of their time complaining are normally part of the problem, not the solution. When the time comes to make things better around your company, they will be nowhere to be found.

Conversely, seek out positive-thinking people. These are the ones who hate to complain and just find a way to get the job done. These are the ones who handle four tasks at once with smiles on their faces, knowing they are going to achieve their goals no matter what. You will naturally attract these people with your positive attitude.

Remember that no matter how successful a person is chances are they got to where they are by being positive and polite, and they will appreciate being approached by a similar person. Seek out this type of person, but remember that if you maintain a positive cheery attitude you will also attract these people into your life as well.

The John Theory

I want to be careful with this section because John was my business partner and is still my good friend. I love John like part of my family. John is an Englishman who had run his company for fifteen years before I met him and went into business with him. He had periods of great success and periods of downturns.

When I joined him and his company he only had three employees. To some degree I feel that fate brought us together. At the time, I had a business investor with me, and we were looking for a company to buy for me to run. I remember to this day calling from a pay phone at a Burger King trying to set up a meeting with John. To make a long story short, my investor wasn't interested in John's company, but there was something there that interested me. I cut a deal with John, and five years later we sold the company and both semi-retired.

John and I had strengths and weaknesses that blended perfectly. He was a very detailed-oriented person, and I was the visionary. I used to say that John had the magnifying glass and looked into the company with a very close perspective, while I had the binoculars and looked into the future. I couldn't see up close, and John couldn't see very far away. Together, John and I had the perfect ingredients for a partnership that was very successful.

John was a very misunderstood person. Many people considered him rude and short-tempered. Because I was in control of my attitude I was able to work with John long enough to understand that he was just misunderstood. He might come across at times like a pit-bull, but inside he was a little puppy dog. Sometimes what he would say wasn't really what he intended. John wore his emotions on his sleeve. I'm still not sure if it was his English up-bringing, his personality, or both. He spent much of his day riding the roller coaster of life and the emotions that can come with it. He was being silly one minute and totally beside himself the next..

I've met people like this in life, and I put them in the category of "having their world tuned to a different frequency" than the average person. What that means is they are seeing and hearing the same information as the rest of us, but they process it a bit differently and their output doesn't always match what we expect. I put many engineers and software programmers into this category. They aren't natural-born salespeople with the ability to communicate on many different levels.

Here's an example: Have you ever been typing something on your keyboard—your thoughts very clear in your mind, just typing away not looking at the screen, and then you look up and see gobbledygook on the screen and realize that your fingers were in the wrong position on the keyboard? This is a clear example of how you thought you were very clear with your thoughts and intentions, but they just didn't come across to the rest of the world the way you intended. As a matter of fact, the rest of the world had no idea what you were talking about.

Sometimes this happens in life when a person attempts to get a point or action across, but for some reason either they don't have the talent or, for the moment, their brain just doesn't have its fingers on the correct keys. What they lack are communication skills. They are sending one signal, but the person on the other end of the conversation is receiving another signal.

The key for those of us who are attempting to be in control of our attitude is to truly see the person within, and in my situation with John, be there for him to help filter information to the outside world.

The point I'm truly trying to get across is sometimes negative-sounding people really don't mean to be negative, it's just that they can't help it. These are people who will never succeed in most sales jobs. However, we need to be aware of them and realize that sometimes if you get to know them, you just might realize that they have hidden attributes that could benefit your future.

In my case I can say that I know that I would have made it in life somewhere, somehow. But in the case of growing and selling the business that John and I ran, that would not have been possible without the combination of our differences. So when I say that you should ignore negative people, remember not to pigeonhole everyone you meet as either simply positive or simply negative.

Sometimes that positive person will reveal themselves as a fake in the future. It is easy at times to appear positive, but over the long run those fakes will prove themselves as liars, cheaters, or con artists.

John comes across as a negative person at times, but he has a heart of gold and is a good person. Over the long haul, being a good person will always win even if you might not come across as the most positive person in the world all of the time.

It's Not What You Say; It's How You Say It

I've long been a believer that you can do and get almost anything you want in life if you don't repel people or make them defensive. We all know people who always scream and demand things. When they ask for something or tell you to do something you just want to throw them in a lake or walk the other way.

My wife and I have always had this discussion about certain people in life. When we realized why we were upset, it wasn't what they said, it was how they said it. So to be a good salesperson, you of course, never want to repel a good customer or colleague. Never burning bridges no matter what happens in life is one of the keys to doing good things and avoiding doing those bad things that will come back to haunt you.

We have to remember not to repel people unless we mean to. We also have to be sure to realize that some people aren't aware of how they are coming across and may not necessarily intend to come across so gruff. It is this power of understanding that can help us control our attitudes.

So the next time you have to ask for something sensitive or deli-cate, remember there are many ways you can come across. You can quite often get what you want and still have a friend at the end. "It's not always what you say, it's how you say it."

Launching Your Ship into Orbit Theory

Sometimes in life all we need to do is either quit going in the wrong direction or start heading in the right direction. I like analogies, and the one that comes to mind is a spaceship up in space in a gravity-free environment that, once started in one direction, keeps heading in that direction until the motion is changed by an outside force.

If you can find the little, easy things in life to do everyday "a little bit over a long period of time," I'm convinced your little spaceship will head in the right direction and you will be heading towards your destination, or destiny.

We are all traveling to a place in time. Some people have no idea where they are traveling. Some people know exactly where they are going. The important issue here is to understand what direction your ship is heading in.

Don't fret if you feel you are far away from your destination. Find joy in knowing that your ship is pointed in the right direction. You will ultimately reach your destination, "a little bit over a long period of time."

Not Afraid of Failure

I learned in golf that many people aren't good players because they are more worried about hitting a bad shot or what can go wrong than they are about hitting a good shot and being successful. I'm sick and tired of hearing, "I can't believe I'm hitting the ball so badly. I was hitting it great on the range." The reason for this difference is that on the range there isn't a consequence for hitting a bad shot, so they are freely swinging, just like they should be doing out on the course.

This reminds me of the sales reps who are afraid to call on the "big" account because they fear there is already too much competition. This is negative thinking, and I can assure you that most all large companies are searching for the best and most reliable suppliers. Don't be afraid to fail—even say to yourself, "I'm not afraid to make a great sales call." When I'm on the golf course in a big tournament, I will often say to myself, "I'm not afraid to make a good shot."

Here is the common theme of this book. It is normal to feel afraid to make the big sales call or call on the leader of the company. Those things that are "normal" are the path of least resistance, which is where the normal herd of salespeople will be heading. Separate yourself from the herd, and you will be one step closer to reaching your goals. Don't be afraid to take risks. If you believe in yourself you will be helping out your future customers in the long run.

No Faking Please

Having a good attitude has to come from the heart. You can't fake a good attitude, or those "in the know" will sniff you out and throw you out the door. The good positive attitude has to come from all of the pieces we are putting together that will exude in your soul.

If you can start to control your attitude, keep from losing your temper, get in great shape, and "do the right thing," then you will create a genuine positive attitude that will shine for all to see. This is probably where the idea that you must love yourself before you can love others came from.

Find out what it takes to get you going. It might be a morning run, meditating in the morning to put things in perspective, or working hard to find joy and to appreciate what you have and the opportunities before you.

To be positive we must have faith and hope for the future. To have faith and hope for the future we must put ourselves in the position to head down the road towards success, "a little bit over a long period of time." To find out where you want to go you must first find out where you are.

If you find that you are faking a positive attitude, then you need to dig deeper into your current situation and accept the point you are at, whether you like it or not. This is a deep thought, but we "are where we are."

Once you can accept your personal reality then start doing something to put yourself on the road to a more positive life, either adding many of the positive directions I've mentioned in this book or eliminating many of the negative issues in your life.

Chapter 4

Rationalize

Rationalizing is an art form just like controlling your attitude and turning a negative situation into a positive situation. I've often said that I tend to think of myself as more of a philosopher than a motivational speaker. It is my belief that we must understand why we do the things we do and why we want to react the way we do and more importantly find tools to assist in controlling our minds and reactions. Sometimes that answer for me is rationalizing.

We only tend to appreciate most things in life that we've either had to work for or we have lost. If everything came easy in life then we would all have everything and nothing would mean anything. How's that for deep thinking? If you think about that statement then you might start to realize that if the only way to appreciate things is to not have those things or to fear losing those things, then you can begin to understand how we can make that hard journey seem more pleasurable. The key is to truly appreciate things and realize how lucky you are to have them. Things are just things, having the ability to be successful to achieve your "things" is what we are striving for.

You've heard the terms "spoiled brat" and "everything handed to him on a silver platter." Kids today who don't work for anything and are given everything set themselves up for disappointment in the future. Real life isn't made up of having everything we want, and more importantly it surely isn't about getting everything we want handed to us on a silver platter.

I live in a neighborhood where most of the parents are well off, and the kids growing up here have had every toy imaginable handed to them. In one sense you could argue that it is a good thing that expectations for a high standard of living have been set, but the downside I have noticed with many of these kids is a smug attitude with absolutely no respect for "real life."

Many of the parents in my neighborhood often joke about our kids not growing up in the "real" world. We say this because most of us grew up in middle-class America and feel fortunate to be where we are today. Kids today have the expectation that money is no object and the belief that material wealth is the key to happiness and success. They think if we need more money then we just go to the money machine to get more out.

Personally speaking, my kids are probably spoiled, but I would like to say that my wife and I have worked hard to instill certain middle-class values in them. We don't have everything we want, and we watch every penny and live within our means. My kids have the sense that there is a limit to what money can buy.

The point of this chapter is to make you all attempt to appreciate what you have once you get it, and to get you into a frame of mind that most things are only temporary, whether they are money or health. One of the keys to life is to appreciate what you have and to enjoy the journey getting there.

The Theory of Opposites

I have been able to explain most situations in my life by comparing them to their opposite. For instance, our minds would not know what love is if we didn't have hate. We wouldn't know pain if we didn't have pleasure. We wouldn't know hot if we didn't have cold; we wouldn't know rich if we didn't have poor; and so on.

Sometimes we have to know the bad side of things to appreciate the good things. There is a fine line between "freaking out" and understanding the opposite, but it is important to be cognizant of the opposite when your mind naturally wants to take the easy way out. By freaking out I'm referring to a neurotic behavior. For instance, we all get upset with our kids for many of the normal things that kids do. Sometimes it drives us to the edge, and we feel we have just had enough. Most of the things our kids do that drive us crazy are exactly the same things we did that drove our parents crazy. Using the opposite theory, I have often found that I can find joy and pleasure when my kids drive me to the edge.

All it takes to realize how much we really love our kids (or family, friends, etc.) is just to watch the news and see the examples of family tragedies that strike across the country. Whether it is a kidnapping or horrible car wreck, you can always find a way to appreciate just how lucky you are to have a smart-mouthed kid with a bad attitude who is healthy and safe at home.

Again I want to stress that you must be careful not to drive yourself into a tizzy by thinking about all of the horrible things that could happen. The point is to realize what you could lose and, more importantly, to appreciate what you have. Appreciating things in life is one of my personal secrets of happiness. It's sad to see people who are always in a bad mood when they have been blessed with much in life and should be grateful for those blessings.

On that same note I want to stress a belief that all human beings should have. We all like "things," and many of us appreciate how fortunate we are to have things; but I strongly believe we need to draw a huge line between things and people.

I don't care how nice your things are—your car, your house, or whatever. They are just things, and things can be replaced no matter how rare or valuable. People, of course, can't be replaced, and therefore must be appreciated on a much higher level. So do me a favor, next time your eighty-thousand-dollar car gets a little scratch on it, please put it in perspective. It is just a material thing, and even though it is nice and pretty, it can be fixed or replaced. Work very hard to not feel love or emotions for material things. Try to keep things in perspective.

If you get emotional about your things then you better be prepared for an unhappy life because things always break, get stolen, need to be replaced, and consume time and money. The more things you have the more hassles you will have in life. Things can be nice; they can make life convenient and more pleasurable at times, but they are not a means to an end. I'm convinced when we are all lying on our death beds we won't be concerned with where all of our things are.

Summing up the opposite theory, you can make a game out of not being upset or depressed about things. Consider how things could be worse, and you will realize how fortunate you are. There is almost always someone who is less fortunate than you.

When you are feeling depressed or down, focus on many of the little things that we all take for granted. The ability to walk, to see, to hear, and even to talk are all things we take for granted. There are many people out there less fortunate than us who would give anything to see the beautiful trees and flowers, to take a walk, to have a nice dinner, or to do many of the things you enjoy on a daily basis.

When you are at your wits end with your kids, who are driving you to the edge, consider all of the parents out there who can't have kids. Many have tried and tried and tried to no avail, while so many of us had beautiful, healthy children without really even trying.

The opposite theory can be like an antidepressant pill if you will just consider how fortunate you are to have what you have, and realize how lucky you really are. There is almost always someone in a worse situation than you are. Feel lucky that you still have a chance to make things better; it is the only way to move forward.

We Are Always Going Somewhere

Life is always changing. If life isn't going somewhere then you are dead. If you are dieting, you rarely are ever at perfect equilibrium. You are always either getting fatter or trying to get thinner. When using "a little bit over a long period of time," it is important to feel that we are moving in the right direction. Now, sometimes we might take a step back to take a few steps forward, but as long as we feel like we are moving forward or there is hope to move forward our minds can remain happy and optimistic about the future. One example might be holiday eating. We might overeat for a few days but then we are right back on track. We can realize that "a little bit over a long period of time" will start to compound as the years go by, and we will ultimately reach our destination.

When I look at my financial situation I just want to keep improving year after year. We want to feel like we will be ahead of where we started. It doesn't matter if you are dirt poor; if you are less dirt poor than you were last year then you can feel good about the progress you have made.

When I trade stocks it is amazing to me how the mind can work when it handles losses. It is very common for most investors to not feel that they have lost money until they have sold their stock at a loss; but that is dead wrong. You have lost money and whether you like it or not you are where you are. You may trick your mind into hoping and wishing that things would turn around and save the day, but the bottom line is you have less money than you started with no matter how you look at it.

I have proven to myself that if I realize that I am in a bad trade, I should sell that trade at a loss. Then I have experienced immediate relief by eliminating that bad trade from my life, and I know that I am that much closer to getting into a good trade. I almost always forget about that trade, and my mind is free and open to think about "good" trades that will ultimately get me to my goal. You can relate this to your everyday life. Get out of bad situations and spend your time on positive situations that will move you closer to your goals.

Sometimes it isn't how much we make or how fast we make it that is important, but rather just that we continue to make the correct decisions. Then we are heading in the right direction. Over the years during rush hour around the Atlanta area, I've noticed that as long as the traffic keeps moving, even if it is only going a couple miles an hour, most commuters will feel pacified that they are making progress. If the traffic comes to a screeching halt and stops, most commuters become agitated and upset that they aren't making progress. Even if traffic picked up after stopping they still feel the impact of not making progress, and it is the same with life.

It isn't the pace of our progress, it is just the direction of our

66

progress that is important. Sometimes our progress will be fast, and other times it will be slow. Feel happy that you are moving in the right direction and remember that one thing leads to another. Even though at this point in time you may not know what new opportunities lie ahead, those opportunities will appear on the horizon if you just keep moving forward. Doors will magically open if you just keep trying. I can guarantee one thing: if you quit trying, you will never reach your goals. In golf if you leave a putt short it will almost never go in the hole; such is life.

Find Joy

Probably one of the hardest things to do is to find joy in the mundane and ordinary periods of life. Much like attempting to control your attitude, finding joy is another avenue of hard work that will bring a realization and perspective to your life that will put things into order. Unless you are one of those rare people in life where you are happy 100 percent of the time, finding joy during down periods is something that takes hard work. Don't get me wrong here. It isn't that we can't have down times and not be up all the time; it is just that many times we can find joyful feelings in our situations if we will just work at it.

Remember what I always say about hard work, it is those times in your life that you consider hard work that are your opportunities to separate yourself from the crowd. As I've said many times, this hard work or separating yourself from the "ordinary people" is a culmination of the small things that help make us successful. We need to associate this so called hard work with the process of assisting us toward our goals. This hard work is seeking pleasure.

Nowadays, when I try to find joy in my life, it is normally on my morning jogs. On those days that I don't feel like running, I use the theory of opposites to find motivation. I start to think how lucky I am to be able to run. I think of all the handicapped people who would do anything in this world just to be able to run. Then I feel privileged and realize that if I don't run, I'll be wasting an opportunity. Taking advantage of opportunities is one of the tickets to our future success.

I find joy in appreciating nature. Try looking at a beautiful sunrise or the spring flowers to see if you can find some joy. Imagine how lucky you are just to be able to see, think of all of the blind people who would pay millions just to see a sunset.

When I pass people on my morning run, I try to give a friendly smile or wave. It is amazing to me how you can influence people to be friendly and how it helps create a joyful mood for you that will carry you through the day and keep life and the simple pleasures in perspective. I mean, we could all be dead tomorrow, and I'm sure that if we knew for sure that we were going to die tomorrow we would soak in all of the beauty of nature. So why not try to feel like that every day. Try to find something that will bring you joy. It might be feeling healthy, giving your wife or child a hug, or something as simple as helping a friend in need.

Chapter 5

Finding Your Potential

If you believe that "everything is relative," you are not surprised to find that potential can vary greatly from one person to the next. My view on potential is that it is a tragedy to waste it. I base my expectations for my children on my perception of their potential. For example, if my child is only capable of getting B's while giving 100 percent of her effort, than I need to set my expectations at a level that will be satisfied with B's. However, if I'm convinced that my child should be getting A's and she is coming home with B's, then I'm going to be very disappointed with my set expectations and my child's performance.

In the business world most bosses and managers aren't too worried about your potential. You either perform or you are gone. You have to start being your own boss and realize to some degree what your potential is. Look deep inside and think about what your goals are. Remember, if you aren't stretching your boundaries in life, you are dying or, at least, getting worse.

We have to understand that it never ends; the process of pushing will last most of our lifetime. It doesn't mean that we have to hate the process. Remember the hard work is the fun part because we are separating ourselves from the pack. Hard work is the vitamin we take everyday.

When you think about finding your potential I want you to think about two things: what can you get rid of in your life that is suppressing your potential, and what can you add to your life that can enhance your potential? I can't think of anything worse in life than living my life knowing that I should have done something or could have done something that I didn't do. Find your true potential and hopefully you will live your life without any regrets. Finding those answers is the million-dollar solution.

It might be your diet, your lack of exercise, your attitude, or your sleeping pattern that is suppressing your potential. You need to take an honest look at your life to find out if there are any negative habits or patterns that you can work on eliminating. For instance, instead of coming home and drinking all night, maybe you could exercise instead. What a change that could make in most people's lives.

To find your true potential you need to do some hard thinking. I still work on this quite often and find new ways that I can get better. You need to think this way for the rest of your life to keep growing and adding to your potential. This is why when I speak about my running, I find it humorous to wonder if I am running from something or running to something. The answer is both.

Personally I am 100 percent convinced that my running is the vitamin that will automatically keep me pointed in the right direction. It is my "habit" in life that is the foundation for my attempts to reach my potential. Exercising may or may not be your answer; but what if it is and you aren't utilizing your time to find out. This could be a classic example of not reaching your potential. These are questions you will need to answer for yourself. All I can do is tell you how exercising totally changed my life. Exercising is my drug of choice.

So what changes can you make today to do "a little bit over a long period of time" to become the person you want to be? Here are a few key areas I suggest that you focus on or eliminate if you want to be on top of your game and reach your full potential in life.

Reach down and grab your belly. If you can get more than a handful then this is a great place to start. I'm not here to be a diet guru, but I am here to say that this fat isn't a good thing. If you really want to reach your potential then you need to work on this part of your life.

You will feel better if you eat better and have a more attractive body. I'd say if I have one weakness in life it is my diet. Even though I've exercised over the past twenty-five years, in my opinion, the last major element for my complete success would be my diet. I significantly cut back on eating red meat when I started running back in college, but I have a major sweet tooth as well as a love for gravies and sauces. These are areas I continue to work on, but I've always been about five pounds from my target weight.

I have mood swings like anyone else, and sometimes I realize that I'm attempting to console myself with a huge bowl of ice cream. I say anything in moderation is acceptable, and it certainly holds true when it comes to desserts. I don't believe that to be perfectly fit we need to eliminate all sweets. We just have to control our urge to devour an entire half-gallon of ice cream in one night—"a little bit over a long period of time."

So what can you do "a little bit over a long period of time" to really make a difference in your diet that will last the rest of your life and make a positive difference in your weight?

One philosophy I have in life is everything in moderation. This idea flows with "a little bit over a long period of time," but especially when it comes to dieting. I also hate to use the word *diet* because it means something short-term. We don't want to diet for the rest of our lives, we want to live our lives. So here are a few tips that have worked well for me and will allow you to "have it all." We need to get to our optimum weight and fitness level slowly by modifying our eating habits, so they can become a "way of life" and not a short-term fix that will go away.

Seven O'clock Diet

I've been exercising for the past twenty-five years of my life, so being overweight has never been a huge problem. I played basketball three times a week for two to three hours at a time for fifteen years, so I could literally eat almost anything I wanted and not gain weight. When I hung up my basketball shoes a few years ago because I was getting too old to keep up with the kids, I immediately gained ten pounds. Since I've never been a big "diet" person, and I refuse to try pills or anything artificial, I've struggled to control my eating habits. When I really started to think about "a little bit over a long period of time" and paying the price, I came up with a few ideas that have worked very well.

One of the problems that many people have is not what they eat, but when they eat it. I found out that most people eat too late at night and even have big meals right before they go to bed. I find that if I eat late at night I sweat, get indigestion, and wake up feeling almost fat. After listening to my body, I came up with the seven o'clock (OK, I'll use the word) diet. This means I eat normally throughout the day—eating breakfast, lunch, an afternoon snack if

I want, and then dinner with my family around 6:30 to 7:00 PM. But, after my dinner I say to my family, "I'm done." It was not always easy not having that bowl of ice cream or that late bowl of cereal. At least I only have to work on three to four hours per day of not eating—from seven at night until I go to bed around eleven. That is all I have to concentrate on. When I am sleeping, I actually get a "bonus" diet because my body is still working on a stomach that isn't full.

It is amazing how quickly you can lose weight and wake up being able to feel your ribs when you use this method. Think about it. If I quit eating by seven, get up in the morning at six thirty, have my morning coffee, and put the kids on the bus, by the time I go for my morning run and have breakfast it is nearly ten in the morning. So I have literally gone for fifteen hours without eating, and for me, other than the time before bedtime, it has been "easy." So again this is one of the keys to success, to find ways like this that may work or fit into your schedule. With this method I don't have to worry about exactly what I eat, I just have to worry about "when" I eat. It helps greatly if your spouse will work with you on this diet so you won't be tempted by watching them eat a big piece of cake before bedtime.

Lastly I want to say that even though I use the word *easy,* I only say that because to me it is much easier to sleep while being a bit hungry than trying to go through the day being hungry when you really might need the energy.

Using the "everything in moderation" theory, I only practice this diet Sunday through Thursday. I'm pretty free to go out on Friday or Saturday and do as I want. I might even eat a bit late, even though I know I won't sleep as well and will add a couple of pounds over the weekend. But that is OK because it is only a couple of nights per week.

What's more important is how we eat for the majority of our time. If you just practice the seven o'clock diet five days a week, you will lose weight and eventually find your ideal weight level. You will also find yourself eating a better meal because you know that you are going to need the nourishment over the next twelve hours or so.

I'll end the diet section by stressing again why we should diet and lose unneeded weight. I'm convinced that most health problems in today's society are by choice. Of course there are some conditions we can't prevent. However, we can't worry about that; all we can do is concentrate on the issues we can prevent. Being healthy and at a good weight is better on your joints, blood pressure, sleep, and, most importantly, your mind. It has even been said that being healthy can reduce your risk of certain cancers and of becoming diabetic.

So be honest when you consider this section because as we go down the checklist of areas in our lives that we have control over and can change, we need to really work on paying the price and getting our body up to its potential.

You put the food in your mouth—only you. Don't worry so much about what you put in there, but rather when you put it in there, and I promise you will see some amazing results. I'll expound on this theory later, but remember that "one thing leads to another" and much like a weak link in a chain you must make sure your diet and body weight are not the weak links.

This is an easy change that *you* can make *today*. Make the change, and see the positive results within a couple of days. Start weighing yourself every morning at the same time and keep a record if you must. Have a goal you want to reach (within reason) and make it happen. Leave just a spec of "happy" around your waist, we don't want skin and bones, but if you are exercising as I want you to, you won't have to worry about that. To me there is nothing worse than just dieting and not exercising. Skin and bones with no muscle tone is almost as unhealthy as being grossly overweight.

Having just a small amount of "happy" around your waist is a critical element of my seven o'clock diet. Unless you are trying to break a world record in swimming or you are trying to become the next super model, it is OK to have that occasional piece of cake at dinner, just not after seven o'clock.

The Best You Can Be at Your Age

We can't all be Michael Jordan or Tiger Woods, probably the best there ever were at their respective sports. On a smaller scale, a healthy way to perceive your potential is based upon your age. Since I've been a runner for twenty-five-odd years I know that I can't keep up with the twenty-year-olds, but I can probably beat or keep up with most of the good forty-three-year-old runners out there. So my point here is that when I think about finding my potential, there are two schools of thought: one is finding your true potential mentally and physically based upon where you have come from, and the second is comparing that potential within your age group.

I truly believe that most of us can keep getting smarter and gaining wisdom well into our eighties and even nineties, but physically we all know that we will have reached our limits somewhere in the early to late thirties. So even though we know that our physical limitations will diminish over time, we still can grade our physical condition by comparing ourselves to others in our age group.

Haven't you heard someone say, "Boy, he looks great for being fifty years old!" Now what does that really mean? It may mean the person they are talking about would not look great compared to a twenty-year-old. But when looking at the average fifty-year-old, the person still looks like a kid. This fits in with the "everything is relative" theory.

Now some of us are just born with great genes, and others aren't. There are certain things we can and can't control—that's life. But we can control what we eat, how much we eat, whether or not we exercise, and, most importantly, how we look at life.

I have always found it interesting to watch a news report about some thirty-nine-year-old guy who just got his fourth DUI and is being put in jail for the sixth time for repeated felonies. It appears obvious to me just looking at this person's picture that this person has lived a very negative and hard life. It amazes me at times how old these people look. As I utilize my "you're competing with people your own age theory" and look at this person, this thirty-nine-year-old person looks like a sixty-year-old.

Then you look at the successful CEO who is sixty-five and appears as fit and happy as can be. This person has lived a positive life with a great attitude, and it shows. I've seen these successful sixty-five-year-olds look as good as average forty-five–year-olds.

Good luck only runs so far. I can assure you that part of the equation for the successful people, as mentioned in many of the topics I discuss in this book, are the things we have control over but have to work hard to maintain, "a little bit over a long period of time." When you are working hard and attempting to reach your goals, remember to be the best you can be for your age.

Falling Off of the Wagon

As we try to exercise regularly, eat better, sleep better, and feel better, it is OK to fall off of the wagon or have a short relapse once in a while. Nothing serious, mind you. Those of us seeking true success would never do something as stupid as doing drugs or getting so drunk that we might do something very stupid. What I'm talking about is on a much lighter scale.

Sometimes in life we just reach a point at which we are tired, maybe a bit depressed because things haven't gone our way, and maybe it is just our down cycle or bio rhythm low cycle. Whatever the case, I have found that if done in moderation falling off of the wagon can have a positive impact once you get back on the wagon. To be in shape you must understand what it is like to be out of shape. It's pretty hard to get out of shape in just a day or so, but you would be surprised how your mind will start working if you suddenly start to feel that you are losing something that you have worked very hard for.

You can only fall off the wagon after you have truly been on the wagon. You have to have achieved a good level of mental and physical fitness. For me, once in a blue moon, like every few months, I'll just buy a big bag of peanut M&M's and go to town. The whole point of this exercise is moderation. I don't mean moderation for that particular day or night; I'm talking moderation because you have been good for a few weeks or even months.

Because I have been exercising my body and mind for so many years, I have found it extremely healthy and rejuvenating to fall off the wagon and just pig out on something for a short period. Almost always after I have one of these episodes, I will have more passion and desire to get into even better physical and mental shape.

Remember that one of the keys of life is "everything in moderation" which is very similar to "a little bit over a long period of time." It is OK every once in awhile when the morning comes that you feel a bit tired and you feel you "deserve" to take the day off from jogging or whatever exercises you regularly do. Personally I may miss about one or two jogging days per month. Sometimes it is just because I'm very tired and busy. Other times it is because I may have a conflict with one of my children's activities. The point is don't stress out about missing a day now and then. It is OK if it is only now and then, and that on your normal workout schedule you are good 95 percent of the time.

Like anything in life, don't go to the extremes, and remember that you are going to be working out for the rest of your life. If one day it doesn't work out, remember that two hundred years from now no one will care that for some reason you couldn't work out on that particular day.

On the other hand, if you take more days off than you work out, that is a problem, and you will never reach your full potential. It is up to you to decide how badly you want this. We don't want to get to the end of our lives with many huge regrets. Trust me when I say I'm sure that if you are successful in your career and you have a massive heart attack in your forties or fifties, then you will have a major "regret" that you didn't take advantage of being able to get out there and start exercising today "a little bit over a long period of time."

Build That Habit Theory And The 10 Minute Challenge

Part of this section is a bit of a repeat of the message in my running section, but I want to expand on how important building the habit of exercising is in the beginning. It is more important than the exercising itself. If you can't find a way to build up the habit of exercising it will just be a passing fad in your life, much like clothing or a silly short-term diet. To make it a lifestyle, something you are going to do for the rest of your life, you will have to ingrain the **habit** of exercising.

Most things in life we don't do on autopilot unless we build a habit. Some habits are good, some are not good. We want to focus on adding those good habits in our lives and getting rid of those bad habits. When I speak of adding good habits one of them, of course, is exercising.

I can't tell you how many times in the past twenty-five years I've heard people make a New Year's resolution and go out full tilt trying to exercise. They fall off the wagon or completely quit exercising because their subconscious mind finds ways to not let them exercise, because then they won't have to commit to the process and feel the pain. I could see it coming. I saw that look in their eyes just before they proclaimed to the world that they were going to the gym everyday for the next fifty years and would get into the best shape possible. Their expectations were set too high and they hadn't built up the habit of regularly exercising.

Well the proof is in the pudding, and if all of America exercised then we wouldn't have to see the fat bodies walking around the shopping malls across the country. Try it sometime. Just go out to a mall, sit down, and do some people watching. I've done this with my daughters just to demonstrate how most of America looks. I don't have a scientific percentage to offer, but in my own opinion I would say that nearly two thirds of America is overweight. Those who aren't overweight seem to be naturally slender, rather than looking like they could run a 10K race. If you want to separate yourself from the pack just walk through a mall and see how you compare. Don't get me wrong, I don't feel that everyone should look like a supermodel. We were all given a specific genetic fingerprint to work with. Being big doesn't mean that you aren't in great shape and living up to your potential. Some people are born with big frames, some with small frames, no matter what shape you are, you need to be in great physical shape mentally and physically to live up to your full potential and get the most out of your career and life.

You won't get in shape overnight, but you can start down that road today. Eventually it will lead you to the path of greatness, whatever your greatness is will be up to you to decide.

The point I must get across to all of you who currently don't have a habit of exercising regularly is this one thing: Don't worry about the exercise itself and all of the great things it can do to change your life. If you really want to exercise for the rest of your life, be in the best shape possible, find self esteem that you never knew that you had, feel like you are closer to God, and incorporate all of the positive attributes that I spoke about in my running chapter, you will need to focus on one simple element— developing the habit of exercising. Before you can work on the physical side of running or exercising, you must develop a habit of getting out there and doing it. If you don't develop the habit first, then you probably won't exercise for the rest of your life. It will just be a fad that will fade away.

Developing the habit is a bit like getting your spaceship into orbit.

If you can develop the habit, then it will become a life force of its own. It will guide you to your destination as you simply keep on with your habit. I mentioned this in the running section in this book, but I want to stress again how important building the habit is versus the pure joy of exercising, or for that matter that hatred of exercising. So here is what I want to strongly suggest as loud as possible. If you don't have any physical ailments that should prevent you from exercising in the first place, then I want you to do this simple trick. Tell your mind that you are going to go jogging (or whatever exercise floats your boat) for just ten minutes five days per week for the next thirty days. If you can convince your mind that your goal is to reach thirty days then you will have "tricked" your mind into launching your exercise ship into orbit and from there you will start experiencing life changing forces that you have never been able to dream about. Most importantly you will have developed the habit which will be ingrained in your system to keep you from falling off the wagon. After you develop the habit of exercising, it will be more painful to your mind to not exercise than it will be to sleep in and eat doughnuts for breakfast.

For the first month, don't even dare go more than ten minutes or you will be missing the point. I'm looking at you directly in your eyes, and I want to say this again. Trust me, I've been a nonstop runner for over twenty-five years, and I've seen all types of people try and fail to develop the habit of exercising. If you cheat even once by going more than ten minutes during the first month, then you are risking getting physically worn out which will allow your subconscious mind to explain why you should not exercise. Do you get the message? Do I need to repeat this again? For thirty days please don't deviate from the ten-minute exercise session, and I promise you that you will develop a habit that will change your life for the better, for now and for the rest of your life.

Just to be clear and annoying I must say this one more time. Don't push yourself until your muscles get tired and sore because this will give your mind a genuine pain-avoidance reaction on which to base other reasons to not get out there and exercise. You may feel as though some people are going to laugh at you and call you a wimp, but please trust me. I'm a serious, dedicated runner, and I've seen person after person try to start jogging, but it is normally over within a few days or weeks, sometimes even in a few hours. If you are not planning to get in shape and enjoy the benefits for the rest of your life, then why bother at all? Not me, I'm going to be doing something until the day I die. Maybe then I'll even be running up in heaven, who knows?

I want you to keep coming back to this chapter if you must and remember that your mind is going to play many, many tricks on you to avoid the pain. This is an exercise in faith. If you've never exercised regularly for years and years, then you have to understand that you don't exactly know what I'm talking about. If you really want to change your life for the better; if you really want that fountain of youth; if you really want to have more energy than your competitors; if you really want to eat better, feel better, look better, and have your planets aligned perfectly everyday, putting you on the path to greatness and your true potential, then you will heed my warning. For the first thirty days, do not work out a minute more than ten minutes, or I will assure you that you won't even get onto the wagon. I want you to work out either every other day or Monday through Friday and take Saturday and Sunday off for the first thirty days.

After thirty days you will be hooked and can start adding a minute a week or whatever you desire as long as you don't overdo it. Remember, I've been jogging for over twenty-five years, and I'm still only jogging for around thirty minutes per day. "A little bit over along period of time" will add up and pay you dividends for years and years to come. Sorry for being redundant regarding building the habit, but I feel this is one of the most important aspects of this book in changing your life for the better.

I'm a Regular Type of Guy

My wife and I debated this subject many times as she pleaded with me to not include this section. Maybe it's a guy thing, but one of the things I'm most proud of with my running schedule is one side effect that is an attribute to regular exercise. I'll just get to the point. I'm regular every morning to the second. I always say, "It's a wonderful thing." I don't want to go into great detail on this subject, but when listing the many great physical and mental benefits of running, I put being regular right up there near the top.

It goes without saying that using the drafting theory during this special time of the day is obvious. I've read many a book this way by just reading about five minutes per day—"a little bit over a long period of time."

Maybe my priorities are skewed, but nonetheless, I wanted to share this important part of my life. Here's to hoping that if you become a regular exerciser that you will experience this wonderful side effect as well. Enough said.

Chapter 6

Golf and Life

I'd probably be remiss if I didn't include a chapter about my golf experience. I have golfed almost every day for the past seven years. This is a dream for most people, and I realize that. I have been trying to point out many lessons about life, and now I want to show how the great game of golf reflects those lessons. Matter of fact if this book "A little bit over a long period of time" is successful I'm planning on putting out a golf book from an amateur's perspective.

I had always said the goal I had, if I could retire early, was to get good at golf and try to make the senior tour by the age of fifty, which at the time was thirteen years away. Now that I'm forty-three, have given my all to the game of golf, and have gone from a fifteen handicap to as low as a four (from the back tees), I can clearly say that this dream will probably never come true. Believe it or not, I think I'm all right with that realization.

Sometimes in life we just have to face facts. I do believe there is an outside chance that if I went to a golfing school for a year, I might find a way to be a horrible senior tour professional, but that just doesn't excite me. Sometimes in life we have to readjust our goals and modify them over time to fit our current situation and needs. Sometimes we just have to face reality. This doesn't mean, however, that we can't find great things that have come from our attempts to reach our goals.

I have met so many wonderful people during the past seven years. I've played with several hundred different people and have become good friends with many of them. None of this would have been possible without my obsession with the game of golf.

I also learned that sometimes things go your way, sometimes nothing goes right, and once in awhile you just get plain lucky. Sounds a little bit like real life, doesn't it?

I know deep in my heart that this great game of golf is leading me somewhere. It teaches me how to control my attitude and how to learn many things about other people and how they react to different situations.

I'm at the point now that I think I can become scratch from my course from the back tees and be very competitive with most players; and that may be good enough for me. I now have the dream of giving motivational speeches around the country, finding some time in between speeches to play golf, and getting to meet many new and wonderful people. In my opinion, I don't think you will ever get to know a person as well and as fast as playing a four-hour round of golf with that person.

Getting up on that first tee before a round is the feeling that we should all have when we start our day. We can make birdies or bogies, but we should have the anticipation of making this the best day of our lives. Every morning, I say to my seven-year-old when I get her out of bed, "Let's make this a great day." It is that feeling of hope and anticipation of good things coming our way that fuels and recharges our batteries for each new day.

You can learn all you want to know about a person by playing golf with them. Most importantly you can observe how they handle adversity. I'm convinced if I ever find myself in the position again where I have to hire people, that I will take them golfing to see how they handle the bad shots and the good shots, as well.

I've seen so many people who are club throwers or who give primal animal screams when they make a bad shot. It is almost hilarious to watch the wild out-of-control actions from some people. These people definitely are not in control of their attitudes and, at times, appear to be torturing themselves by playing golf. Who would want to do that? I've learned that most of these reactions are twofold. One is that many people just don't know how to control their attitudes, and others just have their expectations set way too high.

I don't think that I would like to be in business with a person who cheats in golf or throws a club every time things don't go his way. Aggression is fine, but it needs to be controlled. I'm convinced the only time you really need to show aggression in life is in self-defense from physical harm. Other than that, controlling your attitude and thinking about a way to turn the situation into something positive is the way to go. Not only are most people who lose control of their attitude probably acting like fools, but also they are ruining the experience for their playing partners. Losing control of your attitude on the golf course is just a selfish behavior.

I don't want to sound hypocritical. I've thrown one club in my life, and I've lost my cool with a few playing partners when certain things got out of hand. The point I repeat a million times in this book is that controlling your attitude is hard work, and hard work is the way to separate yourself from the herd and get ahead in life.

If you want to practice controlling your attitude, then try your hardest to be good at golf and see how you handle your bad shots.

Just like with bad shots a person's attitude toward good shots is also important. A person who gloats too much and acts like they just won the lottery after making a great golf shot probably has his priorities in the wrong place as well. Everyone likes a winner, but no one likes someone who celebrates too much. Consider this in life, as well as in business. The next time you make that huge sale, don't act like it is a life changing event or you may find yourself not getting many large sales again.

You need to have the attitude that you expect to make the great shot or large sale and you expect to make many more. It used to be that I almost got upset after a large sale because I worried about whether or not I could top that the next time. But that is the attitude that will keep you grounded and still reaching for the stars, while not offending all those salespeople or managers who are still struggling.

In golf you can't change the past. The bad shot has already happened, and there is nothing you can do about it; much like in life, all you can do is try to think about the future and how you are going to try to do better next time. Sometimes it works out and that is great, but many times you don't quite hit your target, but you just keep going.

In golf sometimes you make a very bad mistake and you need to "take your medicine," which means you aren't going to hit a shot on the green. You are just going to try to put the ball back in play on a flat surface so you can take a full swing again. This is a good example of life. When bad things happen, you don't have to try to get back on your feet all at once. Just point yourself in the right direction and take baby steps until you have your footing, and then you will be headed in the right direction again.

The Crone Bounce

Now this may sound a little bit strange, but I have many golfing buddies who swear that my golf balls are possessed. At my country club there is a very famous term called the Crone Bounce. When I occasionally spray into the woods, remember I'm a five handicap, invariably I get the strangest bounces back out onto the fairways.

Whether this is folklore, voodoo, or just plain luck I have no idea. But I can tell you that when I do hit a stray ball that I can almost always visualize it hitting a tree or some other force to bring it out into play. Now don't get me wrong, I don't get 100 percent of the bounces, and maybe I just get the bounces at the right times, but I could find you a large group of people to swear on a bible that my bounces happen too often not to be uncanny. I always joke with them that I was lucky since the week after I was born, when I was adopted.

The point of this little tangent is not to scare people away because they think I believe in mystical events when I play golf. I'm just saying that it is somewhat folklore at my local club, and if anyone doubts me all they have to do is come visit my club and talk to the members.

I relate my Crone bounces to life. Many times things don't go the way we want them to, and it may look like we are heading out of bounds, but when you least expect it and when you are looking for a little bit of help, something or someone steps in to save the day. If you believe in good luck just like positive thinking, good things will happen and good fortune will come your way.

Eighty Percent Theory

Usually in golf the harder you try, the worse you will do. There is a fine line to this theory, but generally the point is that if you swing too hard it is very difficult to get the center of the clubface on the ball. For most people a swing of around 80 percent will achieve the long shot, as well as increasing the chances of hitting the center of the clubface.

I mention this because if you try too hard when using my "a little bit over a long period time" technique you can go overboard and not be in control. Just think about putting 80 percent of your effort into most of the things you do and you will see greatly improved results. Try hard, but not too hard. Stay in control.

Chapter 7

Attitude

About fifteen years ago, my wife gave me a poem or quote written by Charles Swindoll that literally changed my life. As I was searching for the keys to success: working hard, listening to positive affirmation tapes, reading books, and so forth, I read this poem by Mr. Swindoll and the pieces of my life started to fall into place. This poem literally hit the switch that got me thinking about controlling my attitude. It made me realize how important controlling my attitude would be to my life and my future successes.

I had always had a hard time controlling my attitude. I used to have a horrible temper. This was a temper that was normally brought on by a lost love or alcohol. I never considered myself an alcoholic; however, I learned early on that hard liquor and my personality didn't mix well. For the past twenty years or so I've only been a light beer and wine drinker, and, of course, only in moderation.

I've made a few mistakes by saying things that hurt some of the people I loved. Over twenty years ago, I accepted a personal challenge to learn from my mistakes and not repeat them again. At the time I didn't understand the negative implications of not controlling my attitude. I knew that this wasn't the path I wanted to head towards. I rationalized that everything happens for a reason and if we learn from our past mistakes then something good could come out of it.

After this period in my life I knew I needed to control my temper, but I still wasn't connecting the dots to see that I should have been channeling that energy into something positive. After my wife gave me the Charles Swindoll poem, the pieces fell together for me. I wanted to include this poem/quote from Charles Swindoll in this book, however I wrote to him asking for permission and I was denied. I urge you to Google the "attitude" poem by Charles Swindoll and you will easily find it all over the internet at various sites.

Basically the quote talks about how many things happen to us in life that we cannot control. Sometimes things are good and sometimes things are bad. Our attitude is something that we can control if we really work at it. He talks about how important attitude is and we have a choice.

I am telling you all that the choice to make is to have a great attitude and to be in control of your attitude. This takes work and this takes a conscious effort. I've included the last line of the attitude quote because I feel it is so important.

"The only thing that we can do is play on the one string we have, and that is our attitude.I am convinced that life is 10% what happens to me and 90% how I react to it. "

I have given this poem to my family and all of my co-workers. Once a year or so I review it and am amazed at the connection I have with the meaning of this poem. The line that says life is 10 percent of what happens to me and 90 percent of how I react to it sort of sums up one of my core beliefs.

Controlling our attitude takes work and is hard for the normal person. If all the people in the world believed in controlling their attitudes, the world would have very few problems.

For hard-charging executives and salespeople, controlling our attitudes is a daily event. If we are in an executive position, that attitude starts at the top. You cannot expect anything more out of your salespeople and workers than you do of yourself.

If you are a salesperson, then you are constantly bombarded with the problems you have to deal with on a daily basis. Again, it is hard to control our attitudes; but if we can learn that a positive attitude will take us far in this world, we can have fun in the process of controlling our attitudes. Becoming aware of controlling our attitudes is the first step. The next step will be channeling the anger and crazy emotions that will come boiling to the top. Practice controlling your attitude on a daily basis. You will prevent conflict in your life and create a more peaceful existence. Controlling your attitude doesn't mean we still can't be aggressive, it just means that we are going to be in control as we strive to make things happen that will move us closer to our goals.

Thermostat Theory

When you think about things that happen to you in your life, there are certain things that you have control over and others that are out of your control. Much like the above poem states, the only thing we have control over is how we deal with things, and what our attitude toward them is. I often say in this book, it takes work, but of course it takes work because that is the key, the difference maker, that is what separates us from the crowd.

When we are dealing with problems there are different ways to look at things. I remember one example from my former company that really stands out. It is about how we should prioritize problems and how we deal with them. John, my former partner, was a real penny-pincher, which is a good thing, to a degree. These days I'm known as a very frugal person myself, but maybe I learned many of these traits from John. Being frugal was how John was brought up and how he survived with his company during the lean years.

When I came on board and we started expanding the company, we started adding many new salespeople. Some of these salespeople were the real deal and dressed for success. Our sales room was hovering near eighty degrees because John didn't want to spend too much money keeping the place cool. This was a serious problem for us because I literally had good salespeople threatening that they were going to leave the company because they were hot, miserable, and sweating through their nice business suits. I began to see this problem as unnecessary. John was the partner who ran the details, while I was the visionary. It was John's job in the company to watch the pennies, and he had his name on the bottom line, so I don't blame him for being a bit conservative.

Here I had a serious problem which in reality didn't need to be a problem at all. We had the money to pay the bills, but this issue was a high priority on my partner's list of battles. I knew that one way to deal with this problem was to simply use one finger to move this little plastic lever to the left.

However, I became philosophical about this issue realizing how many serious issues in our daily lives would be easy to solve if we could only just move a little lever. Finally John realized the big picture, and that our company was growing rapidly, and he changed his ways and all the sales reps got to get the cool air they deserved. Our little company grew even faster, and the rest is history.

The moral of this story is twofold. First, don't ever make the mistake of letting issues or problems that really aren't that important get in the way of your success. Realize that small issues CAN actually get in your way and slow you down. You need to either get rid of the problem or find a way to resolve it.

Second, if you can control the issue or problem with a simple flick of a switch (i.e., letter, meeting, etc.), don't let this issue fester to the point at which it becomes a cancer. Get rid of it now and free up space for more positive energy.

At times we all end up wasting so much time on negative energy without realizing it. Sometimes stepping outside of the situation and looking in from the outside will help you prioritize your battles and put them in perspective.

Take Some Time

One other hint that I learned from John that helped me greatly was to put some distance between making an important decision. Whenever we were considering a capital investment or other important decision, John would like to take a few days to consider the implications. I was always accustomed to shooting from the hip. I found out that allowing a day or two when making important decisions enhanced the clarity of my decisions. By that time I would often have a perspective on the issue that wasn't available to me when I first confronted the issue or discovered the opportunity.

Sometimes we don't have time to let a few days go by before making a decision. I'm telling you that I learned that there is a great chance that you may feel differently about your decision if you sit on it for a day or so. You will feel absolutely confident that you are doing the correct thing if you just give yourself some time before you make your decision.

Lose Your Temper, Gain Your Composure

Think about this. You lose your temper, you gain your composure. One theme of this book is to consider those aspects of life for which you have to work at it to "control" something. When we think of attitude, losing your temper is surely a negative event. We always want to gain something, not lose something.

If you are in a business situation and lose your temper but your counterpart has not "lost" his temper, I'll bet in most all cases that you are going to lose the battle. Keeping your composure should be something you are proud of. Keeping your composure should almost be a game to you.

Trust me. Golfing almost every day provides me with plenty of examples of how very easy it could be for me to lose my temper. All day long I watch idiots lose their tempers on the golf course and throw club after club. Keeping your composure is hard to do, but you can do it with practice, "a little bit over a long period of time." Keeping or gaining your composure can save your job, your relationships, and even your blood pressure.

The last thing I want to say about controlling your attitude is that I am speaking about controlling your anger. Don't turn into a drone. Live life, laugh furiously and be happy. Control your attitude when you get angry and upset. If you can put yourself in a position in which you can either avoid the situation or turn it into a positive one then you are going to get ahead much quicker in life, even if it is "a little bit over a long period of time." Most of the bad things that happen to us in life will happen when we lose control of our attitude and do something that we will regret.

Forgiveness Theory:

The ability to forgive has changed my life. Without even knowing what I was doing I learned the ability to forgive and to move on. To not forgive is to hold a burden. Burdens are normally negative and are unneeded baggage that will slow us down in our journey towards success.

When I started one of my first companies in 1987 I was 25 years old and I had a partner who was 23. We were both very young in the business world and in life as well. We were great friends and had an exciting view of the future and how great we could make it. We started our business selling computer products on a shoe string.

To make a long story short we had a great little business and we were certainly in the "right place at the right time". In 1987 the computer industry was really taking off and computer networking was the coming rage and we were just moving into that huge growth market.

Because money was tight we were introduced through our accountant to a wealthy widower who was looking to buy into a business. We figured we had the contacts and the energy and she had the money to finance things so it would be a perfect fit. We sold her a third of the business and in return she gave us a 100 thousand dollar line of credit to use in growing the business.

The huge mistake we made during this "deal" was to allow our new partner to take all of the back room operations out of our office and under her control. Now in one sense you can't blame this lady for wanting to have "control" over her investment, but in reality this totally killed the business because soon things started to fall out of control as we didn't have the flexibility to make quick financial decisions that were needed as a small growing entrepreneurial company.

As the business was soon becoming a pain in the butt and after I lost control of my attitude by yelling at this new investor on how in my mind she was "ruining the business" things quickly started to deteriorate. It didn't take long to realize that this wasn't going to work.

This situation even started creating a rift between my good friend and business partner. It appeared obvious to my other two partners that maybe the answer to their problems was to get rid of me since I seemed to be the one complaining the most. I knew in my heart that there was no way I could work under these conditions so I suggested that I leave the business. All I asked is that I was indemnified from any corporate liabilities and all they asked was that I sign a non-compete to not start up a competing business in the area.

Even though I hadn't formulated many of the theories that I currently use in my life today, I knew that my path to success was down another road and I knew that the current road I was traveling was not going to lead me to my destination. At this point I was happy to give up my current dream and ready to move on. I knew I would find my way and I was eager to avoid the pain of being around the current situation.

So here I was, 26 years old, newly engaged and needing to leave the area if I was going to stay in the computer business. I had some decisions to make. The major decision I made internally was to release or forgive my business partners. I did not hold any feelings of anger or resentment. I knew that deep in my heart that I was a winner and under the current situation that it just wasn't "meant to be".

If I had been on the other side of the camp where I was angry and bitter and feeling that I wanted to sue my partners for turning against me, or maybe finding a way to ruin the business and make the situation as miserable as possible, then many negative situations could have occurred.

The moral of this story of course is that I moved on, moved to another state and 8 years later achieved the success I was seeking. This proved to me that I was in control of my own destiny and that the act of forgiveness had allowed me to release my burden which enabled me to rise above my obstacles and move on.

Now that I look back on the situation I have one loud resonating sound that never stops going through my head. When I was considering my options in regards to the wealthy financial partner my wife told me that she didn't think it was a good idea because we would be losing control. I've learned from that mistake and have since listened to my wife, using her as a sounding board when it comes to making major decisions.

On a side note the reality of the business that my young friend and I started is that we were on the cusp of something that could have been very huge. After I moved from Florida to Georgia and was involved in the computer industry I saw many companies that were exactly like the company that my friend and I started. If we had not made that decision to bring on the financial partner I'm still convinced that we would have possibly grown one of the larger companies in the area. Would have, could have, should have is a saying that I often use.

Sometimes things don't happen and we just have to deal with it. The point I want to make is that I made it taking a different route. Whatever happened to my partner might always be a mystery to me. I have absolutely no hard feelings towards either partner because in my mind they did me a favor. Without them I wouldn't have been able to move to Georgia and meet John my future partner where things did work out together. I was able to help John retire wealthy which is something that I am very proud of.

Another quick example of forgiveness has to do with my years of playing basketball. I played basketball at a local gym for 3 days per week for nearly 13 years. This was a big part of my life at the time and was very important to me.

There were often scuffles and little fights at times as the testosterone might be flying a little high. I had set a pick on an opposing player and he didn't like it so he pushed me, I pushed him back and I thought that it was over. Because I had been a jogger I used to be a non-stop runner of the baseline moving underneath from 3 point line to 3 point line. Before I new it as I was running from one side to the next the back of my head came crashing to the floor. The person I had gotten into the pushing situation with, threw out his arm and "clothes lined" me. This is something you occasionally see in football but it is considered very dirty and very dangerous for the person getting clothes lined, particularly when you aren't wearing a helmet.

The next thing I know I'm waking up on the floor and had been knocked out cold for nearly 30 seconds or so. After a few of my friends nearly threatened to kill this guy he was escorted out of the gym and actually kicked out of the gym for a couple of months by the management of the gym.

Playing ball at this gym was very important to me. I got great exercise, got to be around a ton of my friends and "hang out", and got to compete which is something I needed in my life.

I could have handled this situation in many different ways. I could have called the police and pressed charges. I could have gone after this guy and attempted to beat the crap out of him, or maybe I could have released the situation and burden and forgiven this guy because I realized that if someone had to actually clothes line a guy for setting a pick then they must have some real issues in their life. In a way I turned my thinking into feeling sorry for him. I knew his brother and was somewhat friendly with him so I knew that he wasn't just a thug but a guy who might have some issues who probably made a mistake.

Well the day came a couple of months later when the fellow who clothes lined me showed back up at the gym. Because I had already forgiven him and moved on I felt no anger or resentment towards him. Actually because I had moved my mind towards feeling sorry for him I wanted to help him. Now what I did next probably shocked him because if you can put yourself in his shoes he as well is probably wondering what is going to happen. I'm sure in his mind he was still ready to fight.

I approached him "playing a little game" and had a stern look in my face and moved up to him and then stuck out my hand and said, "Welcome back, good to see you again". He seemed a bit amazed and relieved at the same time and he actually smiled a bit and said something like "good to see you as well". Since that time we were fine and actually played well together and against each other. What I accomplished by forgiving him was to not let him ruin a part of my life that was a "happy place". I didn't need to go to the gym where I was having a great time and be worried about seeing someone who I hated or had an uncomfortable feeling about. I had totally released my burden and once again I had a feeling of happiness and serenity at my gym.

The ability to forgive should be important in all of our lives. If you have done something wrong towards someone then by all means you should approach them and tell them you were wrong. If they don't accept your apology then really the problem is theirs, not yours. On the other hand if someone has done something bad towards you then the greatest thing you can do if you are upset about the situation is to forgive them, even though they might not be the type of person to feel sorry for what they have done. It really doesn't matter if they feel sorry or not, that can just be icing on the cake. What is really important is that we don't hold those feelings of anger, jealousy and resentment that can eat us up inside.

Chapter 8

Expectations

Life is all about expectations and how we react to those expectations. I first discovered my theory of expectations while learning about Wall Street and the financial community. In the stock market, if you try to rationalize why stocks do certain things, you might go nuts. A stock with great blowout earnings drops 10 percent on the news. A stock that loses millions of dollars for the quarter sees its stock gain 10 percent. Of course the expectations were built into the stock, and the stock price acted according to those preset expectations.

So how can we relate what happens on Wall Street to real life? First we have to determine what our expectations are. There is a saying that came from A.L. Williams: "All you can do is all you can do." If you are attempting to use all of your potential, then "all you can do is all you can do."

What this means is that you have to accept what happens and go with it if you have tried as hard as you can. It is a way to accept what happens and to set your expectations at a certain level. I use this saying often to myself and my family when we try as hard as we can and things just don't go our intended way. "All we can do is all we can do". It is a way of just accepting reality.

If you think about it there are really three scenarios. You meet your expectations, exceed them, or fall short of them. How you react to each of these scenarios can vary, but it is something you need to understand. I have learned to not let my expectations run rampant. If you routinely fail to meet your expectations, you will spend most of your life being disappointed. On the other side of the coin, you don't want to keep your expectations too low or you will never meet your highest goals. Maybe the point is to think about and be aware of your expectations so you can analyze your reactions and adjust accordingly.

My wife and I have learned that when we go out to see a movie that someone has just raved about, we often are very disappointed in the movie. Our expectations were set so high that we could only be disappointed. On the other hand, I can't tell you how many times we have rented an off-the-wall, you-never-heard-of-it movie and were pleasantly surprised by how much we enjoyed it. Our expectations were so low.

First, ask what you want in your life, your career, and your health. My answer is that I want to live up to my potential and get there "a little bit over a long period of time." I expect that if I put out a small bit of effort each and every day, over time things will add up to become great. My expectations aren't to have this happen overnight. If great things happen I put them in check, and if bad things happen, I just keep going and doing what I call "wading through the mud."

Top salespeople don't become that way overnight, and if they did I would only be impressed if they could keep up that pace over a long period. Look at some of the greatest NFL running backs, such as the late great Walter Payton. He was my favorite because of his work ethic and attitude. He became the greatest rusher of his time, and he did it by getting a bit over one hundred yards per game over many games. So he did it "a little bit over a long period of time," adding up the yards like throwing money into the bank. Over his thirteen years in the league, he became one of the game's greatest runners.

Salespeople should view their work life like a good running back would view his. Do the things everyday that will keep you in shape, and keep running the ball, adding up the sales everyday. Over time you will be known as a producer who can deliver consistent results, and you will be much more valuable to your company than the flash in the pan salesperson who gets lucky with a large order one month and then falls to the bottom of the pack the next.

Year after year, Walter Payton showed up to training camp in better shape than the year before. Salespeople and executives should take a lesson from Walter Payton and always keep trying to get better, even if they are already the best in their company.

All you can expect to be is the best you can be. A major theme of this book, is finding your potential, "a little bit over along period of time." Your expectations can come from the relativity of your past or from your vision of your future.

What will make you truly happy? For most people it isn't finally reaching your goals. Remember, when the day comes that you have achieved all you can achieve as a person, that is the day you will begin to get worse.

I'm a firm believer that the mind is something that can always learn and grow "a little bit over a long period of time." Almost every single day you need to concentrate on your menial chores that will add up: keep your mind, your body, and your house in order. Keep those planets aligned and keep pushing to further your life and career to reach your full potential.

New Salesperson Mud Theory

Invariably when I would witness a new salesperson attempting to start a career and make a go of things, I would almost always notice one unique element in their progress. After the initial emotional high of either getting pumped up or excited about the future, they would almost always reach a point in their progress at which they felt like they wanted to give up. They would start losing faith in their abilities and success rate. I call this hitting the wall or wading through the mud. It happens in almost all new ventures in life. This is the part of the process that separates the weak from the successful.

The most important lesson to remember during this process is that if you hang in there, you will come out through the other end of the tunnel and see the light. I did it when I started out in sales. I wanted to give up and find a "safer" way to make a living. However, I kept knocking on those doors and hearing those rejections and then boom, I got a huge order from knocking on that one last door.

I have recently gone through this with my golf game. There were times when I had spent so much emotional and physical effort that I thought I was wasting my time trying so hard. During this period, when I was a worse golfer than I was a year earlier, I kept reminding myself of the "new salesmen mud theory." To make a long story short, after another six months of struggling and trying to play through it, I came out the other end, and now I'm on my way to becoming a scratch player.

My golfing experience is much like my sales experience. Much of life and golf is confidence. Since I had never been a great golfer, I wasn't comfortable shooting a low score. I would tense up and push too hard hoping things would work out if I was having a great round. Quite often, I would bogey or double bogey the last few holes because of this attitude. Now that I'm becoming a much better golfer, I see myself getting much less nervous coming down the stretch if I have a good round going. This is called experience and something that must be earned with hard work and taking risks.

So what is the real moral of this story? Remember that if you really want to be good at something, whether it is sales, golf, or even parenting, you have to pay the price. Most importantly, you will reach a period during which you lose hope and faith. You will feel like you are walking through deep mud, and it will be hard to move forward.

You have to remember in the back of your mind that this is where you pay the real price that will reap dividends in the future. Nothing comes easy. If you just hang in there and keep trying, you will find a way to get through this period and you will become the person you want to be. Keep in your mind that this period and process is normal, even though it may not be fun. Please trust me in this. Hear me loud and clear. This is one of the secrets in life. When others are quitting because they want to avoid the pain, just a bit more effort and faith on your part will take you to your promised land. I have seen it done many times, and I am a perfect example of this theory in my own experiences. Keep the faith and separate yourself from the crowd. Don't ever give up and when you hit the hard part, the mud, remember that your promised land is just a short distance away if you will only put on your hip boots and wade your way through that mud.

Tenfold Theory

The world and the business world run in a certain order. If you are willing to play the game, look the part, act the part, and run under the corporate social guidelines, you can quickly climb the corporate ladder.

When I started my first company, I learned quickly that many people running businesses are not exactly truthful and good people. I do believe that there are more good people than bad, but in business, there are many people who are willing to take shortcuts to get ahead unethically.

I am convinced that in the business world if you do something bad, whether it is lying to a customer, stabbing a co-worker in the back, or misleading your boss, bad things will come back to you tenfold in short order.

People don't like to be taken advantage of or misled. Most good people who have bad experiences with certain people will go out of their way to warn other people, vendors, and customers about you. Bad things will come your way at least tenfold from the original bad act that you started or created. Keep this in mind next time you think you want to cut some corners or tell a little white lie in business.

Throw the truth out there, gently if needed, and get it over with. Let the chips fall where they may. You may endure some short-term pain, but in the long run you won't reap the bad effects of the tenfold theory.

Conversely, if you do something good for a customer or co-worker, the tenfold theory works on the positive side as well. Unfortunately, the return isn't as quick or as great with the positive effect as it is with the negative effect. Nonetheless, if you sing in tune with this book of "a little bit over a long period of time" you will reap the positive benefits of a positive action over time. Your honesty and integrity will grow, and over time you will ride the wave of the tenfold theory in the proper fashion. Do the right thing and protect your integrity with all of your might. Over time your great attitude, generosity, and integrity will start creating positive windfalls over your lifetime. Do the right thing.

Acceptance

Once you accept the fact that life works "a little bit over a long period of time" you can then begin to adjust your expectations. Adjusting your expectations is a large part of the battle. Find joy and happiness in just moving forward, in making progress even if you think it may be small. Small is a relative term and remember that the small movements forward are the ones that are going to add up over time.

Expand your mind to create unique ways to allow actions to add up "a little bit over a long period of time." I'll be interested to hear about the many ways to incorporate "a little bit over a long period of time" that people have come up with in their lives. I hope many people who read this book will share these ideas. I want to hear how people come up with ideas like my drafting theory, which allows me to easily build a habit of doing my sit-ups and push-ups. If you get a chance please come to my web site, www.phillipcrone.com, to tell me about your ideas so that I can share them with other people who might be interested.

There have to be hundreds of other "a little bit over a long period of time" ideas that can help us build up our lives and become mighty oak trees. Accept the fact that we can control certain things in our lives and that there are many things in life we can't control. Acceptance is just living with that reality and making the best of the situation.

Analyst Report

I've traded stocks for many years. I am familiar with the many analyst reports that come out for each given stock. I relate these reports to our own lives. You should be your own analyst and should take the time to document your past, your future outlook, and your strengths. Try to come up with a stock price for yourself. Are you an undervalued small cap or are you a blue chip company that keeps producing positive earning reports and consistent dividend flows?

Looking at yourself and your life from a third-party perspective can offer views into your life that you probably weren't aware of. View your life the way you think a stranger would view your life if he got to interview you and find out about all the particular secrets and aspects of your life. This is an honest way to identify habits to get rid of or come up with positive habits to add to your life.

Personal Affirmations

I say certain affirmations when I run. I'm a huge believer in affirmations because they plant seeds in your subconscious mind which will help propel you to reach your goals in the future.

What are affirmations? They are thoughts or ideas of who we aren't today and who we would like to become. I feel affirmations are close to praying. If you can take the time to think about and visualize the person you want to become and then put those pictures into words, you will be programming your subconscious mind with the information it needs to reach those goals.

There has been much research done over the years on the power of the subconscious mind over the conscious mind. The debate continues about how the process really works, but I have no doubt the subconscious mind is really the driver of our lives. The conscious mind is more like the robot who has been programmed by the subconscious mind. The only way we can really tap into the subconscious mind is by putting ourselves in a position to make our subconscious mind listen to us. The way to tap into this hard-to-reach wizard is through affirmations.

By repeating the goal or repeatedly visualizing the person we would like to become, we slowly build an imprint that will force the subconscious mind to find a path to our goals. The subconscious mind won't listen for long so we must keep repeating these affirmations over and over every day until we reach our goals.

My two girls are the joy in my life. Even though I'm directing this book toward salespeople and executives, I would say that my daughters and my wife understand my philosophies as well as anyone. For the past few years I have extended my affirmations to my daughters at the morning bus stop. When the bus arrives, I give each girl a kiss and a hug and repeat the following, every single day, "Have a great day. Have a good attitude. Get good grades. Be nice to everyone. Eat a good lunch." Then, as a joke referring to the movie *Freaky Friday*, I always end with, in a sarcastic voice, "Make wise choices."

My girls are humored by this, and on the rare occasion when I almost forget to say these affirmations they remind me, commanding, "Dad, say it." I view this now as almost as important as giving them a hug and a kiss and saying goodnight before bed. I'm sure someday that they will pass this along to their children, and at least they fully understand my expectations for them each and every day. On a side note, when I wake up my little daughter each morning I always say to her, "Let's make this a great day." I know that over time I am programming her mind with my expectations.

Everything Has Its Place

I'm not what one would call a neat nick. I do, however, like things to have their places. This is an important aspect of life. If you spend most of your time looking for things, instead of using your brain for its true power—creating new positive ideas—your mind won't have time to come up with those powerful thoughts that will propel you closer to your goals. Get organized in your life so that many of the things you do can be run on autopilot.

Always keep your keys and wallet in the same exact place. Everything has to have its own place. Keep the junk and clutter out of your life. If you don't use it often and still don't want to throw it away, put it away in a box somewhere so it is not getting in the way of the stuff you use. It is so important to not have to worry about finding things that it is incredibly important to always have a system for your important things.

As you develop your "a little bit over a long period of time" systems in your life you will discover ways to organize yourself for these routines. I can give you one simple example. When I go for my morning jog I always have my running shoes in the same exact closet. I grab my sunglasses from the same storage place above the door. When I run, I grab my car keys with my house key from a drawer where I always store my keys. I actually even run the same exact route for at least five years, so I don't have to worry about how far I have run or where I'm going to run. I normally say the same affirmations at the same spots on my run. Again, the key to all this neurotic behavior is that I can free up my mind to wander and to think about the things that will help me get ahead in life. If I was spending all of my time wondering where I put my keys, then I wouldn't have time to let my mind do what it does best, and that is think.

When I'm finished with my run I have the same exact routine which is also a factor of "a little bit over a long period of time." I spend a few minutes at the same place outside my house stretching, then I come inside and put my wet shirt in the same place, away from the normal laundry so my wife doesn't have to bother with my stinky clothes. I put my sunglasses back in the same storage spot, throw my keys in their drawer, and then get a big glass of water and take my 1000 mg of vitamin C, at the same time Monday through Friday.

This is a good time for me to take my vitamin. Since I have performed this routine for over twenty years, I don't have to worry about whether or not I have taken my vitamin for the day. I may get about one cold per year, but I'm convinced my vitamin C, along with a positive attitude, helps keep my immune system strong. I'm drafting on my run and this process is done automatically, because I have made it part of my routine and it has become a habit over the years. Vitamin C is the only vitamin or nutrient that I take.

So, in short, go around your house or your office and find a logical place for everything, so that you can free up your brain for its important work. If you have the room, buy as much of the stuff as you can of the things you use regularly. I normally buy about a five-year supply of vitamin C, shampoo, toothpaste, deodorant, and so forth. This is in line with my theory that if you free your brain from the petty details that clog it up like a stopped up pipe, it can think more freely and creatively.

Consider all the times in your life when you wasted time or missed deadlines because you were looking for things. See if you can come up with a system that will put things on autopilot. The more systematic you can make some chores in your life, the more time you will have to be creative.

Write It Down

I'm convinced a brain and a computer are very similar. You only have so much space on your hard-drive (brain), and you only have so much Random Access Memory in your computer. If you spend all of your time trying to remember what you need to remember, your hard drive (brain) will become so cluttered and filled up with useless information, that you will have no space left for what really leads to success in life, and that is creative thinking.

With the technology today we have personal digital assistants to remember all of those petty things that we need in life like dates, numbers, passwords, and so forth. One way to really expand the mind is to carry a little pad of paper around with you. Out of the blue you will start to get little flashes of creative thoughts, and this is when you should write them down and put some thought into them.

Once you begin to relieve your mind of these great ideas as they come, you will create more space for more great ideas. You will be able to come up with more ideas about how to create things, change things, and so forth. Spend time just trying to think about things and picture where you want to go in life. If you can see where you want to go your brain will start forming a plan and mapping a path to your destination. Spend time each day just thinking "a little bit over a long period of time." I don't know about you, but my mind is so busy thinking about different ideas that I will forget these ideas if I don't write them down. Sometimes I have found that simply having a piece of paper handy to write things on excites my mind into spontaneously creating those ideas, so I can feel the pleasure of writing them down.

Conclusion

It is my true belief that we will never find all of the answers in life. I certainly don't know all of the answers, and I am also convinced that the answers for me will be much different than the answers for others.

We may learn the answers when we get to heaven, but for now, life is a journey filled with lessons every single day of our lives.

As we travel through life we develop a belief system based upon our experiences and our reactions to those experiences. Sometimes those experiences can shape us in a way that can either do long-term harm or good, depending on the situations and how we react to them.

I'm hoping some of you will relate to my way of thinking and incorporate this type of thinking into your own lives. As I said in the beginning of the book, I would be surprised if anyone would agree with 100 percent of what I have written and what I currently believe. If the average reader can find a few of my philosophies or tips that can change their lives for the better, then I will feel as though I have achieved my objective—to help others.

For the average salesperson or executive who truly wants to achieve their fullest potential and who wants to get better every single day of their lives, I am fully convinced that many of my ideas or theories in this book will benefit you and your friends. For the person who may not be on the fast track just yet, I'm also confident that a few of my ideas, like controlling your attitude and getting healthy, will lead you to bigger and better things in the future.

I also want you to understand that my ideas aren't set in stone. I even plan on modifying some of my beliefs over time as my own personal experiences shape and mold my future. What I really want you to learn from this book is that if you don't believe in one of my ideas, that is great because you have your own belief system, and it may work great for you. I'm hoping that when you find an idea of mine you don't agree with, you will agree that controlling your attitude is something that may work for everyone, even you. It doesn't matter what religion or political party you belong to. I'm convinced that if we can control our attitudes and find a way to turn obstacles into positive opportunities, then maybe we have found one of the "secrets" of life. It's too bad the rest of the world doesn't believe in this philosophy because if they did we would have a much safer world to live in.

It's out there if we just go out and grab it. First, we must have those dreams, and then we have to find the desire to make them come true. All dreams and passions can come true if we just "find a way." Sounds simple but "finding a way" is a combination of persistence, desire, motivation, and many other elements of success we have all heard and read about.

I will end this by saying that I hope I can motivate some of you to start building the habit of exercising and aligning your planets. Plant the seed for your mighty oak today. Time is running out!

Make it happen today! Live your life to the fullest and don't have any regrets. Good luck!

Please e-mail me with your comments or suggestions:

phillip@phillipcrone.com

For information on motivational speeches for your business or organization please contact me at the following Web address:

www.phillipcrone.com

Thorlo Testimonial

Phillip Crone 43, Author, "*A Little Bit Over a Long Period of Time*"
"Thorlo has been with me every step of the way"

I retired in 1997 at the age of 37 after selling a successful computer company. I attribute this success to my health, fitness level and attitude. I have been a jogger for over 25 years now and am still going strong at the age of 43.

My most recent venture is a book titled, *A Little Bit Over a Long Period of Time*. I wrote it in order to articulate my attitude, techniques and the importance of health and fitness to anyone looking for the secrets to success that work.

One of the important points I make in the book is that **"Thorlos have been with me every step of the way."** Throughout my years of jogging Thorlos have been the one constant and make my point perfectly about what kind of impact something as simple as the "right" sock can have on your ability to keep your body healthy and your mind sharp when used consistently over time.

As I completed *A Little Bit Over a Long Period of Time*, I approached Jim Throneburg, THOR•LO, Inc Chairman and Owner, with the idea that I wanted to use Thorlos and my experience with them to drive home the point of the title of my book. I could see Thorlos as a key part of my book and speaking engagements. Thorlos perfectly fit the mission of my story and Jim saw the "connection" between "A Little Bit Over A Long Period Of Time" and "Thorlos over a long period of time".

I strongly feel that all Americans should be healthier. I am passionate about sharing my experience with Thorlos, believing that they will have the same positive effect on others' journey to become healthier and more successful. Jim would say, "Thorlos will allow you to enjoy more running life". In fact, I attribute my 25 years of injury free running to Thorlos.

You might wonder how one could be so passionate about a sock, all I can say is that if you've never worn a Thorlos you can't understand what I'm talking about. It's like the *Opposite Theory* of life in my book—-try a Thorlos on one foot and any other ordinary exercise sock on the other. You will experience the Thorlos difference for yourself.

I am so confident that if you try Running Thorlos you will feel the same way I do that I made a deal with Jim, to the effect that every person that comes to the Thorlos website using my special promo code, registers and gives all the information requested, Jim will send you a pair free. Thorlos will even pay for the shipping. (Offer good only for bookmarks included in books bought directly from www.PhillipCrone.com.)

It's time to take the *Thorlos Ten-Minute Challenge* you read about in my book. Start changing your life today!

Visit www.thorlo.com… for more information regarding Thorlos.

For more information regarding my book *A Little Bit Over a Long Period of Time* please visit www.phillipcrone.com .